The London Cheese & Wine Guide.

Edited by
Lucy Gregory and Jeffrey Young

Author: Allegra Strategies

Writers: Sophie Austen-Smith
and Lucy Gregory

Wine writer: Matthew Jukes

Photography: Maximilian Gower

Design & artwork: John Osborne
and Andy Mac Manus

Website: Tim Spring and Lee Goldsmith

Publisher: Allegra Publications Ltd

D1340986

Published in 2012 by Allegra Publications Ltd, No.1 Northumberland Ave, Trafalgar Square, London, WC2N 5BW

Visit our website:
www.londoncheesewineguide.com

All information was accurate at the time of going to press.

Published by *Allegra* PUBLICATIONS Ltd © 2012
No.1 Northumberland Ave, Trafalgar Square, London, WC2N 5BW

Foreword

Wine and cheese are a magnificent and time-honoured union, revered around the world.

In the UK, we have not always tasted cheese and wine at their best. But our appreciation of these specialised and fine regional products has come a long way since Abigail's Party. In part, this is due to a recent resurgence of artisan cheese and wine, made to exceptionally high standards by masters of the trade. This focus on quality over mass-production, combined with huge advances in transport, allows us to enjoy a staggering variety of cheese and wine in perfect condition.

The sheer amount of choice can be daunting and it means good advice is essential. The London Cheese & Wine Guide will arm those entertaining at home with the tools to carry off the smartest cheese and wine events imaginable. And if you are out for the evening then look no further to find an array of restaurants and bars, excelling in the world's most exquisite drink and its gustatory counterpart.

The experts behind this book have the peerless knowledge to lead you around the capital with unerring accuracy and into the arms of the finest purveyors of cheese and wine. It is in these venues that you can fall in love with cheese and wine for the first time or lose yourself to an existing passion.

Cheese and wine are back in fashion and taking London by storm. This book will put you ahead of the trend and inspire you to expand your experience of these two sophisticated, gastronomic delicacies.

Matthew Jukes
Wine Writer

Contents

Introduction

Welcome to The London Cheese & Wine Guide – the first ever guide to London's top cheese and wine venues.

We think good cheese and wine should be accessible and universally enjoyed. By providing straightforward information about cheese and wine, we aim to dispel the misconceptions that can make these products intimidating.

London has an exceptional variety of cheese and wine venues to suit different occasions and accommodate every budget. The London Cheese & Wine Guide features the best of these venues from across the capital. Discover a fantastic shop just around the corner or a perfect bar on the other side of town. Wherever The London Cheese & Wine Guide takes you, don't forget to be adventurous and ask the experts for advice.

Allegra Strategies is a well-established leader in research and business intelligence to the food and drink industry in the UK and Europe. It has drawn on this research as well as countless other sources (including industry experts, blogs, general community views and staff of the cheese and wine venues) to compile The London Cheese & Wine Guide.

ÔTES
RHÔNE
LLAGES
ERVAIS

ALIEU

DOMAINE
SARCIN
CÔTES DU RHÔNE
FAMILLE EVESQUE

2010

DOMAIN
HAR

CÔTES DU RHÔN
MIS EN BOUTEILLE À LA PROPR

About the Guide

The London Cheese & Wine Guide is an independent publication. Every venue featured in The London Cheese & Wine Guide has been visited by our expert team and chosen because it is one of the best cheese and/or wine venues in London.

We have rated the top 5 venues in each category that deliver a "wow" factor to the customer. Elements which have been taken into account include: range and quality of cheese and/or wine, product presentation, venue heritage, innovation and customer service.

It was not considered fair to assess market stalls on these criteria so they have not been rated.

Cheese Pricing

Mature Cheddar prices refer to Cheddar which has been aged for at least 12 months. Parmigiano-Reggiano prices refer to Parmigiano-Reggiano which has been aged for at least 24 months.

Symbols used throughout The London Cheese & Wine Guide

Cheese

 Vegetarian cheese

 Accessories and accompaniments

 Hampers sold

 Cheese wedding cakes

 Wine sold

Wine

 Enomatic sampling available

 English wine

 Organic / biodynamic wine

 Wine accessories

 Cheese platter recommended

General

 Gift vouchers

 Disabled access

Cheese

An Introduction to Artisan Cheese

Artisan and Farmhouse Cheese

The venues we feature in this book pride themselves on selling artisan cheese, but what does this mean and why is it important? Artisan cheese is locally produced and made on a relatively small scale, using traditional methods with minimal mechanisation. The result is a high quality product, which has been crafted with care and attention by expert individuals who have a genuine understanding of their trade. All handmade cheeses are slightly different, even if they have been made by the same person on the same day. So with every artisan cheese you taste, you are experiencing something unique.

A factory-made cheese, on the other hand, differs very little from one piece to the next. This consistency is an advantage because you always know what the cheese will taste like. However, even a good example of factory-made cheese will be less complex than its artisan counterpart and you are less likely to find a truly sensational cheese.

You may hear the words "artisan cheese" and "farmhouse cheese" used interchangeably but they are not quite the same thing. Farmhouse cheese is made on the cheesemaker's farm using milk exclusively from his or her own animals. Non-farmhouse cheese can be made using milk from several different farms. Usually, farmhouse cheese is also artisan.

Cheesemaking in Action

Treating the milk

To start the cheesemaking process, the milk's acidity must be increased to prepare the milk for curdling. Historically, this occurred by leaving the milk to sour for a period of time. Regulation and consumer demand means that this is often no longer possible, so a starter culture is added to the milk to help the process along.

Curdling

Once the milk's acidity reaches a suitable level, rennet is added to the milk. This causes the milk to curdle, which is the separation of milk into curd (solids) and whey (liquid).

Draining and shaping

The curd is then placed into a mould to drain any excess whey. For softer moister cheeses, the curd may simply be scooped or layered into a mould. For harder cheeses, the curd is cut before being placed in the mould. Some hard cheeses are pressed to draw out even more whey. Once it has been taken out the mould, the cheese (no longer referred to as curd) is either washed in a brine solution or rubbed with salt. Only then is it ready to be matured.

Maturation

During maturation, cheese is kept in temperature and humidity controlled conditions until it achieves the optimum texture and flavour. Most cheeses are turned periodically during the maturing process to ensure the correct distribution of moisture. Some cheeses will undergo further washing in a brine solution to become "washed rind" cheeses. This is also the stage where some cheeses are pierced with needles, allowing air to enter the cheese and develop a blue mould.

Pasteurisation

Pasteurisation is the process of heating milk to a high temperature to destroy any harmful bacteria found naturally occurring in the milk. Unfortunately, the pasteurisation process also kills benign bacteria which lend flavour to the cheese. For this reason, artisan cheese is usually made with unpasteurised milk although some artisan cheesemakers choose to use pasteurised milk because it is more stable than unpasteurised milk and has greater consistency in quality. Certain cheeses, such as Stilton, are required by law to be made with pasteurised milk.

Protected Designation of Origin (PDO)

You may have come across letters, such as "PDO", "AOC", "DO" and "DOP", after the names of certain cheeses. These denote that the heritage of the cheese is protected so only cheese that has been made in a specific way and in a particular region can be sold with that name. This is a way to ensure that the quality and characteristics typical of these cheeses are preserved. The different letters reflect the protection marks of different countries. "PDO" stands for Protected Designation of Origin and is a European Union mark. "AOC" stands for "Appellation d'Origine Contrôlée" and is the French appellation mark. "DO" is a Spanish mark that stands for "Denominación de Origen", whilst "DOP" is the Italian "Denominazione di Origine Protetta".

Specialist Shops

London's specialist cheese shops sell the best of British and Continental cheese, which is lovingly cared for by passionate and knowledgeable staff. While buying your cheese, take time to learn about the products from these experts and experiment with new flavours and textures.

Androuet

Old Spitalfields Market, 107b Commercial Street, E1 6BG

This franchise of the French fromager, Androuet, brings a touch of Parisian chic to Spitalfields Market. The cheeses are predominantly French (as one would expect) but a partnership with Paxton & Whitfield means there is a substantial British offering as well. Owner Alex Guarneri matures his cheeses to perfection in cellars underneath the Market, before bringing them upstairs to line the shop walls. The adjoining restaurant, run by his brother Leo, provides an ideal pit stop for a glass of wine and a cheese board while you contemplate purchases.

OPEN
Mon-Sun.   10:00am - 7:00pm

OVERVIEW
First opened
2010
Owner
Alex and Leo Guarneri

CHEESE
No. available
80
Countries of origin
Britain, France, Ireland, Italy,
Scandinavia, Spain, Switzerland

PRICING per 100g

Brie de Meaux	£2.07
Mature Cheddar	£2.31
Parmigiano-Reggiano	£2.85
Stilton	£2.09

CONTACT
020 7375 3168
www.androuet.co.uk
ag@androuet.co.uk
⊖ / ⇌ Liverpool Street

Beillevaire

7 Montpelier Street, SW7 1EX

OPEN

Mon-Sat. 10:30am - 7:00pm
Sun. 10:30am - 4:30pm

There are 400 French cheeses to explore in this shop so take your time, ask lots of questions and enjoy being surrounded by so many of the world's finest cheeses. If you are in need of an instant fromage fix, you can create your own cheese board from the shop's selection to eat in store. Don't forget to try some of the Beillevaire family's own butter and yoghurt, made on their farm in the Loire. The shop's décor is an interesting mix of the slic and modern with the jovial, which adds a touch of fun to your visit.

CONTACT

020 7584 1231
www.fromagerie-beillevaire.com
f.beillevaire@beillevaire.com
⊖ / ⇌ Knightsbridge

Other London locations
Borough Market

OVERVIEW
First opened
2010

CHEESE
No. available
460
Countries of origin
Britain, France, Italy, Spain

PRICING per 100g
Brie de Meaux	£2.60
Mature Cheddar	£4.03
Parmigiano-Reggiano	£4.09
Stilton	£3.36

Cheddar Deli

108 Northfield Avenue, W13 9RT

With so many different artisan cheeses available in London, you might think England's most famous cheese had been forgotten. At this shop, however, Cheddar is the main event. You will always find Westcombe, Montgomery's, Cave Matured from Cheddar Gorge, Keen's and Isle of Mull in the counter. There are also up to five "guest" farmhouse Cheddars selected by owner Brent Wilkinson, depending on seasonality and availability. The shop offers a wide range of British, Irish and French cheeses, as well as artisan charcuterie and delicatessen.

CONTACT

020 8810 0690
www.cheddardeli.com
⊖ / ⇌ Northfields

OPEN

Mon-Wed.	9:00am - 5:00pm
Thu-Fri.	9:00am - 6:00pm
Sat.	8:30am - 5:30pm
Sun.	Closed

OVERVIEW

First opened
2011
Owner
Brent Wilkinson

CHEESE

No. available
130
Countries of origin
Britain, France, Ireland, Spain, Switzerland

PRICING per 100g

Brie de Meaux	£2.10
Mature Cheddar	£1.65 - £2.60
Parmigiano-Reggiano	£3.25
Stilton	£2.10

The Cheese and Wine Company

72-74 Station Road, TW12 2AX

OPEN

Mon-Tue & Sat.	10:00am - 6:00pm
Wed-Fri.	10:00am - 10:00pm
Sun.	11:00am - 3:00pm

Owner Steve Parker runs his business on three principles - taste, provenance and knowledge – all of which are evident when you visit The Cheese and Wine Company. Tasting is encouraged and in one visit you can collect all you need for a cheese and wine evening, including stories about your purchases and the people who made them. Fans of smoked cheese will love Smoky Vicar and Smokehouse Blue, locally made and available exclusively at this shop.

CONTACT

020 8941 7758
www.thecheeseandwinecompany.co.uk
taste@thecheeseandwinecompany.co.uk
⊖ / ⇌ Hampton

OVERVIEW

First opened
2010
Owner
Steve Parker

CHEESE

No. available
200
Countries of origin
Britain, France, Germany, Ireland, Italy, Netherlands, Portugal, Scandinavia, Spain, Switzerland

PRICING per 100g

Brie de Meaux	£2.40
Mature Cheddar	£2.40
Parmigiano-Reggiano	£3.20
Stilton	£2.20

Cheese at Leadenhall

4-5 Leadenhall Market, EC3V 1LR

OPEN

Mon-Tue.	9:00am - 5:00pm
Wed-Fri.	9:00am - 8:00pm
Sat-Sun.	Closed

Cheese at Leadenhall is a great location for cheese fans in the City. The venue is primarily a cheese shop but also encompasses a cheese café and wine bar. Head over during a lunch break or after work to pick up some of the shop's wonderful cheeses or unwind with a glass of wine and a cheese-based meal. For a romantic date with a difference, pre-book a "cheese tour for two" and enjoy a private tutored tasting.

CONTACT

020 7929 1697
www.cheeseatleadenhall.co.uk
sue.cloke@cheeseatleadenhall.co.uk
⊖ / ⇄ Bank

OVERVIEW

First opened
2005
Owner
Sue Cloke

CHEESE

No. available
150
Countries of origin
Britain, France, Ireland, Italy, Netherlands, Spain, Switzerland

PRICING per 100g

Brie de Meaux	£1.99
Mature Cheddar	£2.19 - £2.49
Parmigiano-Reggiano	£2.99
Stilton	£2.19

The Cheese Block

69 Lordship Lane, SE22 8EP

OPEN

Mon-Fri.	9:00am - 6:30pm
Sat.	9:00am - 6:00pm
Sun.	10:00am - 4:00pm

This shop has an incredible selection of cheeses so you should be able to find exactly what you are after. The owner, Mr Rao, even creates his own cheese called Cibosano (Gorgonzola mixed with Stracchino and walnuts), which is worth a try if there is some available when you visit. The shelves are stacked high with every type of relish, chutney, pickle and preserve imaginable along with a large range of other deli goods.

CONTACT

020 8299 3636

⊖ / ⇌ East Dulwich

OVERVIEW

First opened

1991

Owner

Mr B Rao

CHEESE

No. available

275

Countries of origin

Britain, France, Germany, Italy, Netherlands, Scandinavia, Switzerland

PRICING per 100g

Brie de Meaux	£2.59
Mature Cheddar	£2.49
Parmigiano-Reggiano	£2.99
Stilton	£2.25

The Cheeseboard

26 Royal Hill, SE10 8RT

Royal Hill is a delightful shopping destination where you can buy fresh fruit and veg, meat, fish and cheese in adjoining independent shops. The Cheeseboard is a small community shop where friendly and knowledgeable staff will help you find just what you are looking for, whether it is an old time favourite or something new and unusual. Most of the shop's cheeses are British and French but it boasts a broad range from across the Continent. Of particular interest are the cheeses matured by expert French affineur, Paul Georgelet, and the impressive selection of lesser-known Spanish and Italian cheeses.

CONTACT

020 8305 0401
www.cheese-board.co.uk
sales@cheese-board.co.uk
⊖ / ⇌ Greenwich

OPEN

Mon-Wed & Fri.	9:00am - 5:00pm
Thu.	9:00am - 1:00pm
Sat.	8:30am - 4:30pm
Sun.	Closed

OVERVIEW

First opened
1985
Owner
Michael Jones

CHEESE

No. available
100
Countries of origin
Britain, France, Ireland, Italy, Netherlands, Scandinavia, Spain, Switzerland

PRICING per 100g

Brie de Meaux	£1.72
Mature Cheddar	£1.75
Parmigiano-Reggiano	£2.87
Stilton	£1.80

Cheeses

13 Fortis Green Road, N10 3HP

Mon & Sun.   Closed
Tue-Sat.   9:30am - 5:30pm

This tiny, charming shop in the heart of Muswell Hill has been selling artisan cheese for 30 years. Owner Morgan McGlynn sources her produce from independent producers and is happy to promote more unusual cheeses if they meet her high standards. The shop has an air-raid shelter out back, which makes the perfect maturing room for two of the shop's most popular cheeses - Montgomery's Cheddar and Colston Bassett Stilton.

CONTACT

020 8444 9141
www.cheesesonline.co.uk
shop@cheesesonline.co.uk
⊖ / ⇌ East Finchley

OVERVIEW

First opened
1982
Owner
Morgan McGlynn

....

CHEESE

No. available
200
Countries of origin
Britain, France, Ireland, Italy,
Netherlands, Scandinavia, Spain,
Switzerland

PRICING per 100g

Brie de Meaux	£2.60
Mature Cheddar	£2.40
Parmigiano-Reggiano	£3.46
Stilton	£2.20

....

Good Taste Food and Drink

28 Westow Hill, SE19 1RX

OPEN

Mon-Thu.	9:00am - 6:00pm
Fri-Sat.	9:00am - 10:00pm
Sun.	11:00am - 4:00pm

This delightful shop was opened by Manish Utton-Mishra so he could share his love of quality cheese and charcuterie. Good Taste Food and Drink has already impressed locals with its offering of predominantly British cheese and cold cuts. Highlights include a selection of 15 blue cheeses (all British), Scottish green pepper wild venison salami (the shop's best seller) and Kentish cooked ham.

CONTACT

020 8761 7455
www.goodtaste-fd.co.uk
manish@goodtaste-fd.co.uk
⊖ / ⇌ Gipsy Hill / Crystal Palace

OVERVIEW

First opened
2011
Owner
Manish Utton-Mishra

CHEESE

No. available
55
Countries of origin
Britain, France, Netherlands, Switzerland

PRICING per 100g

Brie de Meaux	£1.95
Mature Cheddar	£1.95 - £2.00
Stilton	£2.25

Hamish Johnston

[TOP 5]
IN CATEGORY

48 Northcote Road, SW11 1PA

OPEN

Mon-Sat.	9:00am - 6:00pm
Sun.	11:00am - 4:00pm

Hamish Johnston has an extensive range of glorious cheeses, meticulously displayed in the spacious counter according to type. Centre stage is given to a beautiful collection of 40 goat's and ewe's milk cheeses from across Europe including the UK. Knowledgeable staff will help you find a new favourite cheese but if you are short on time and in need of inspiration then ask about the weekly featured cheeses. Blackboards behind the counter provide amusement while you browse, with cheesy jokes and trivia.

CONTACT

020 7738 0741
www.hamishjohnston.com
info@hamishjohnston.com
⊖ / ⇌ Clapham Junction

OVERVIEW

First opened
1994
Owner
Mark Newman and Will Johnston

CHEESE

No. available
150
Countries of origin
Britain, France, Ireland, Italy,
Netherlands, Scandinavia, Spain,
Switzerland

PRICING per 100g

Brie de Meaux	£2.20
Mature Cheddar	£1.69 - £2.03
Parmigiano-Reggiano	£2.66
Stilton	£1.82

19

La Cave à Fromage

24-25 Cromwell Place, SW7 2LD

OPEN

Mon-Thu.	10:00am - 7:00pm
Fri-Sat.	10:00am - 9:00pm
Sun.	11:00am - 6:00pm

The cheese-filled windows of La Cave à Fromage are a wonderful welcome to South Kensington, and more than enough to tempt you into the shop. Once inside, you can see the full selection of French and British cheeses set up in an open counter. There is a small seating area in the centre of the shop and what could be better than taking time out from a busy day to enjoy some cheese, bread and a glass of wine in true French style?

CONTACT

020 7581 1804
www.la-cave.co.uk
london@la-cave.co.uk
⊖ / ⇌ South Kensington

OVERVIEW

First opened
2007
Owner
Eric Charriaux and Amnon Paldi

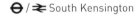

CHEESE

No. available
250
Countries of origin
Britain, France, Ireland, Italy, Portugal, Scandinavia, Spain, Switzerland

PRICING per 100g

Brie de Meaux	£2.50
Mature Cheddar	£2.95
Parmigiano-Reggiano	£3.40
Stilton	£2.50

La Fromagerie

2-6 Moxon Street, W1U 4EW

Owner of La Fromagerie, Patricia Michelson, is a doyenne of the cheese world and La Fromagerie is one of the best cheese shops in the country. The rustic-style cheese room is filled to the ceiling with at least 200 of the finest cheeses, from the well-known to the obscure. The on-site maturing house nurtures the cheeses until they reach optimum condition and can be sold in the shop. It is almost impossible to choose just a few cheeses to take home but you can seek inspiration from the tasting café, which offers a selection of regional cheese boards alongside suggested wine pairings. Many top chefs cite this shop as their favourite cheese venue and La Fromagerie supplies a host of Michelin-starred London restaurants.

OPEN

Mon-Fri.	8:00am - 7:30pm
Sat.	9:00am - 7:00pm
Sun.	10:00am - 6:00pm

OVERVIEW

First opened
2002
Owner
Patricia and Danny Michelson

CHEESE

No. available
250
Countries of origin
Britain, France, Germany, Ireland, Italy,
Netherlands, Portugal, Scandinavia,
Spain, Switzerland

PRICING per 100g

Brie de Meaux	£2.50
Mature Cheddar	£1.95 - £2.59
Parmigiano-Reggiano	£3.59
Stilton	£2.35

CONTACT

020 7935 0341
www.lafromagerie.co.uk
moxon@lafromagerie.co.uk
 / Baker Street

Other London locations
Highbury

Neal's Yard Dairy

6 Park Street, SE1 9AB

Neal's Yard Dairy is the ultimate destination in London for British and Irish cheese. The shop's first class counter hosts cheeses from over 70 artisan cheesemakers, many of which have been expertly matured in-house. The white-washed walls, stone flooring and stacks of Cheddar truckles create an authentic dairy feel. There is even an atmospheric shower in the corner, which maintains humidity in the shop, allowing the cheeses to be left unwrapped. The engaging staff will explain any cheese and always offer you a taster. Owner Randolph Hodgson has played a pivotal role in the revival of British cheese over the past 30 years. Anyone visiting Neal's Yard Dairy will agree that he has done a fantastic job.

Mon-Sat.   9:00am - 6:00pm
Sun.   Closed

OVERVIEW
First opened
1996
Owner
Randolph Hodgson

CHEESE
No. available
80
Countries of origin
Britain, France, Ireland, Italy

PRICING per 100g
Brie de Meaux   £2.34
Mature Cheddar   £2.65 - £3.02
Parmigiano-Reggiano £3.60
Stilton   £2.29

CONTACT
020 7367 0799
www.nealsyarddairy.co.uk
boroughshop@nealsyarddairy.co.uk
⊖ / ⇌ London Bridge

Other London locations
Covent Garden / Spa Road

Paxton & Whitfield

93 Jermyn Street, SW1Y 6JE

OPEN

Mon-Sat.	9:30am - 6:00pm
Sun.	11:00am - 5:00pm

London's oldest cheese shop, Paxton & Whitfield, can trace its origins back to 1742 and has been at its current location since 1896. The quality of the cheese and service remains of a traditionally high standard but otherwise the store offers a thoroughly modern shopping experience. The stunning open counter dominates its recently refurbished black and cream surroundings. New cheeses are regularly introduced and since 2009 a French selection from Parisian fromager, Androuet, has sat alongside Paxton's British offering. The cheeses are matured on-site and sold in peak condition by expertly trained staff. Stylish cheese accessories line the walls alongside the finest biscuits and preserves. This is one of Britain's iconic shops and should be visited by everyone in London, let alone cheese lovers.

OVERVIEW

First opened
1797

Owner
Andrew Brownsword

CHEESE

No. available
250

Countries of origin
Britain, France, Ireland, Italy, Netherlands, Spain, Switzerland

PRICING per 100g

Brie de Meaux	£2.50
Mature Cheddar	£2.40
Parmigiano-Reggiano	£3.20
Stilton	£2.10

CONTACT

020 7930 0259
www.paxtonandwhitfield.co.uk
jermynstreet@paxtonandwhitfield.co.uk
 / Piccadilly Circus / Green Park

Rippon Cheese

26 Upper Tachbrook Street, SW1V 1SW

With an astonishing 500 cheeses, Rippon Cheese has the largest selection in London. The temperature-controlled shop creates the perfect environment for housing every cheese imaginable. If you want to learn more, then book a tour of the store's maturing rooms where you can taste cheeses in different stages of maturity.

CONTACT

020 7931 0628
www.ripponcheese.com
info@ripponcheese.com
 / ⇌ Victoria

OPEN

Mon-Fri.	8:00am - 5:30pm
Sat.	8:30am - 5:00pm
Sun.	Closed

OVERVIEW

First opened
1990
Owner
Philip and Karen Rippon

CHEESE

No. available
500
Countries of origin
Britain, France, Ireland, Italy, Spain, Switzerland

PRICING per 100g

Brie de Meaux	£2.30
Mature Cheddar	£1.46 - £2.11
Parmigiano-Reggiano	£2.92
Stilton	£1.72 - £1.91

The Teddington Cheese

42 Station Road, TW11 9AA

You feel right at home in this small kitchen-style shop, where each type of cheese has its own little cupboard. The Teddington Cheese has a substantial British and Irish offering, from Somerset to Scotland and everywhere in between. The European selection includes some of the finest traditional cheeses as well as a few unusual examples – more adventurous customers could try the pungent U Bel Fiuritu from Corsica or tangy mature Esrom from Denmark.

CONTACT

020 8977 6868
www.teddingtoncheese.co.uk
cheese@teddingtoncheese.co.uk
⊖ / ⇌ Teddington

Other London locations

Richmond

OPEN

Mon & Sun.	Closed
Tue-Wed.	10:00am - 5:00pm
Thu-Sat.	9:30am - 5:30pm

OVERVIEW

First opened
1995
Owner
Tony Chuck

CHEESE

No. available
130
Countries of origin
Britain, France, Ireland, Italy, Netherlands, Scandinavia, Spain, Switzerland

PRICING per 100g

Brie de Meaux	£2.00
Mature Cheddar	£2.30
Parmigiano-Reggiano	£3.60
Stilton	£2.00

Yellowwedge Cheese

6 Crown Road, TW1 3EE

OPEN

Mon.	Closed
Tue-Fri.	10:30am - 6:00pm
Sat.	10:00am - 5:30pm
Sun.	11:30am - 2:30pm

The counter at Yellowwedge Cheese is home to around 140 cheeses at any one time. The British offering is particularly strong but you can also buy diverse cheese from all over Europe. Look out for the shop's unusual speciality, Paški Sir, a hard Croatian ewe's milk cheese. There is no shortage of extras to accompany your cheese either. From boards and biscuits to preserves and pickles, this shop has everything you need for a fromage feast.

CONTACT

020 8891 2003
www.yellowwedge.com
mail@yellowwedge.com
⊖ / ⇌ St Margarets

OVERVIEW

First opened
2007
Owner
David Harries and Philip Brocklehurst

CHEESE

No. available
150
Countries of origin
Britain, France, Ireland, Italy,
Netherlands, Spain, Switzerland

PRICING per 100g

Brie de Meaux	£2.20
Mature Cheddar	£2.10
Parmigiano-Reggiano	£2.60
Stilton	£1.95

Delicatessens

London delicatessens sell some of the world's finest produce. Alongside authentic regional goods and homemade cooked meals, you will find plenty of artisan cheeses often supplied by top London cheesemongers.

Bayley & Sage

[TOP 5] IN CATEGORY

60 High Street, SW19 5EE

OPEN
Mon-Sun.   8:00am - 9:00pm

The abundant display of locally-grown, fresh produce gives an immediate indication of quality at Bayley & Sage. Work your way through the prepared meals and patisserie to the enormous counter packed with 130 cheeses from Britain and the Continent. The large offering means you should always be able to find something new to taste and the notable selection of German and Swiss cheeses is well worth exploring.

CONTACT

020 8946 9904
www.bayley-sage.co.uk
info@bayley-sage.co.uk
 Wimbledon

OVERVIEW

First opened
1997
Owner
Jennie Allen

· ·

CHEESE

No. available
120
Countries of origin
Britain, France, Germany, Ireland, Italy, Netherlands, Spain, Switzerland

PRICING per 100g

Brie de Meaux	£2.25
Mature Cheddar	£2.50
Parmigiano-Reggiano	£2.95
Stilton	£1.95

· ·

Cannon & Cannon

18 Market Row, SW9 8LD

OPEN

Mon.	Closed
Tue-Wed.	11:00am - 5:30pm
Thu-Sat.	11:00am - 11:00pm
Sun.	11:00am - 5:30pm

Brixton Village Market is one of London's newest foodie hot-spots and a fitting location for this "Cheese and Meat Salon". The selection of British-only cheeses may be small but it is well-considered and changes weekly so you will always find something new to try. Either take away your purchases or "build your own platter" of cheese and charcuterie to eat in with a glass of organic wine or a London-brewed beer.

OVERVIEW

First opened
June 2012
Owner
Sean and Joe Cannon

....

CHEESE

No. available
20
Countries of origin
Britain

CONTACT

020 7501 9152
www.cannonandcannon.com
info@cannonandcannon.com
 Brixton

PRICING per 100g

Mature Cheddar	£2.20 - £2.30
Stilton	£2.90

....

Daylesford Organic Farmshop & Café

44B Pimlico Road, SW1W 8LP

OPEN

Mon-Sat.	8:00am - 7:00pm
Sun.	10:00am - 4:00pm

Daylesford Organic Farmshop & Café is a beautifully designed store and with so much delicious produce on offer you will find it hard to leave. Amongst the small selection of familiar cheeses, look out for the ones made on the farm itself with milk from Daylesford's British Friesian cows. There are ten award-winning cheeses in total, including Daylesford's Organic Cheddar, Bledington Blue, Single and Double Gloucester.

CONTACT

020 7881 8060
www.daylesfordorganic.com
thefarm@daylesfordorganic.com
⊖ / ⇌ Sloane Square

Other London locations
Notting Hill / Selfridges Foodhall

OVERVIEW

First opened
2002
Owner
Carole Bamford

CHEESE

No. available
20
Countries of origin
Britain, France, Italy

PRICING per 100g

Brie de Meaux	£2.50
Mature Cheddar	£1.99
Parmigiano-Reggiano	£3.55

The Deli Downstairs

211 Victoria Park Road, E9 7JN

OPEN

Mon-Tue.	9:00am - 5:30pm
Wed.	9:00am - 6:30pm
Thu.-Fri.	9:00am - 7:00pm
Sat.	9:00am - 6:00pm
Sun.	9:00am - 4:00pm

Owners of The Deli Downstairs, Theo and Sarah Fraser Steele, have created an inviting and vibrant shop in the heart of Hackney. The cheese is supplied by Neal's Yard Dairy, Mons and KäseSwiss so you can be assured of top quality produce from across Europe. Choose from a variety of fresh pasta, quiches and breads to have with your cheese for a delicious lunch at home. You can even bring along an empty wine bottle to refill with your choice of house red or white from barrels at the back of the shop. In the summer, take the whole lot to Victoria Park and enjoy over the course of a lazy afternoon.

CONTACT

020 8533 5006
www.thedelidownstairs.co.uk
contact@thedelidownstairs.co.uk
⊖ / ⇌ London Fields

OVERVIEW

First opened
2009
Owner
Theo and Sarah Fraser Steele

CHEESE

No. available
60
Countries of origin
Britain, France, Ireland, Italy, Spain, Switzerland

PRICING per 100g

Brie de Meaux	£2.25
Mature Cheddar	£2.00
Parmigiano-Reggiano	£3.00
Stilton	£2.00

The Gazzano's

167-169 Farringdon Road, EC1R 3AL

OPEN

Mon.	Closed
Tue-Fri.	8:00am - 5:30pm
Sat.	9:00am - 5:30pm
Sun.	10:00am - 2:00pm

This traditional deli has been run by the Gazzano family since 1901 and is a home-from-home for many of London's Italian residents. Come here for Italian cheeses including Parmigiano, Pecorino, Mozzarella di Bufala, four types of Gorgonzola and the best Provolone Auricchio. There is also plenty of authentic olive oil, prosciutto, pasta and every other type of Italian produce you can imagine.

OVERVIEW

First opened
1901
Owner
The Gazzano Family

CHEESE

No. available
45
Countries of origin
France, Italy, Spain, Switzerland

PRICING per 100g
Parmigiano-Reggiano   £2.35

CONTACT

020 7837 1586
thegazzanosltd@btinternet.com
 / ⇌ Farringdon

Gusto & Relish

56 White Hart Lane, SW13 0PZ

OPEN

Mon-Fri.	10:00am - 6:30pm
Sat.	9:00am - 6:00pm
Sun.	Closed

Gusto & Relish sells a diverse selection of 45 cheeses from Britain, France and Italy, mainly supplied by Neal's Yard Dairy and La Fromagerie. Ask about matching cheese and wine or suggestions for combining your cheese with a meal. For an indulgent treat, try the store's Valrhona chocolate truffles, which were star-awarded at the 2011 Great Taste Awards.

CONTACT

020 8878 2005
www.gustoandrelish.co.uk
info@gustoandrelish.co.uk
⊖ / ⇌ Barnes Bridge

OVERVIEW

First opened
2000
Owner
Sally O'Gorman and Richard Lane

CHEESE

No. available
45
Countries of origin
Britain, France, Italy

PRICING per 100g

Brie de Meaux	£2.23
Mature Cheddar	£2.59
Parmigiano-Reggiano	£3.57
Stilton	£2.59

Harrison's Delicatessen & Vintners

60 Pitshanger Lane, W5 1QY

With 100 cheeses and 40 cold cuts, there is no shortage of choice at this friendly Ealing deli. Harrison's range of cheeses from France and Switzerland is particularly impressive - try the hard-to-find Swiss Bergblumenkäse and Stilsitzer Steinsalz for an authentic taste of the Alps. Complement your cheese with a bottle of wine, hand-selected by the Harrison family from small artisan producers around the world.

CONTACT

020 8998 7866
www.harrisonswines.co.uk
sales@harrisonswines.co.uk
⊖ / ⇌ Castle Bar Park

OPEN

Mon.	Closed
Tue.	9:00am - 7:00pm
Wed-Thu.	9:00am - 8:00pm
Fri-Sat.	9:00am - 9:00pm
Sun.	11:00am - 4:00pm

OVERVIEW

First opened
2010
Owner
Belinda Harrison

CHEESE

No. available
100
Countries of origin
Britain, France, Ireland, Italy, Netherlands, Scandinavia, Spain, Switzerland

PRICING per 100g

Brie de Meaux	£2.00
Mature Cheddar	£2.60
Parmigiano-Reggiano	£2.50
Stilton	£2.00

M. Moen & Sons

24 The Pavement, SW4 0JA

Mon-Fri.	8:30am - 6:30pm
Sat.	8:30am - 5:00pm
Sun.	Closed

M. Moen & Sons started life as a traditional British butchers but is now more of a "food emporium". Alongside the stunning cuts of organic and free-range fresh meat you will find charcuterie, cooked meats, dry goods, fresh produce and around 80 cheeses. The cheese selection is classic and predominantly British but look out for the beautifully kept French goat's milk cheeses at the front of the counter.

CONTACT

020 7622 1624
www.moen.co.uk
email@moen.co.uk
⊖ / ⇌ Clapham Common

OVERVIEW

First opened
1971
Owner
Garry Moen

....

CHEESE

No. available
80
Countries of origin
Britain, France, Ireland, Italy, Spain

PRICING per 100g

Brie de Meaux	£2.00
Mature Cheddar	£2.20
Parmigiano-Reggiano	£1.98
Stilton	£1.75

....

Delicatessens

MacFarlane's

48 Abbeville Road, SW4 9NF

[TOP 5]
IN CATEGORY

OPEN

Mon-Fri.	8:00am - 7:00pm
Sat.	8:30am - 6:00pm
Sun.	10:00am - 5:00pm

The MacFarlane's cheese counter is varied, well-organised and has informative labels with tasting notes. Make sure you try the locally-sourced Isle of Avalon, a pungent washed rind cheese made at the farm of British cheese legend, James Aldridge. If you cannot wait to get your cheeses home then create a tailor-made cheese board from the counter to enjoy at one of the shop's outside tables.

CONTACT

020 8673 5373
www.macfarlanesdeli.co.uk
info@macfarlanesdeli.co.uk
⊖ / ⇌ Clapham South

OVERVIEW

First opened
1998
Owner
Robert Marsham

CHEESE

No. available
70
Countries of origin
Britain, France, Ireland, Italy, Netherlands, Spain, Switzerland

PRICING per 100g

Brie de Meaux	£2.55
Mature Cheddar	£2.20
Parmigiano-Reggiano	£3.00
Stilton	£2.10

Mortimer & Bennett

33 Turnham Green Terrace, W4 1RG

OPEN

Mon-Fri.	8:30am - 6:00pm
Sat.	8:30am - 5:30pm
Sun.	Closed

Peer into the cheese counter at Mortimer & Bennett and you will find some very interesting cheeses indeed alongside the usual suspects. Ask about Lou Claousou and Sounal de Hyelzas (two phenomenal ewe's milk cheeses from South-West France) and Rond de Lusignan (a mature goat's milk cheese from Poitou, matured by expert affineur Paul Georgelet). Once you have collected your cheese, take some time to choose from the premium delicatessen which fills the rest of the store to the rafters.

CONTACT

020 8995 4145
www.mortimerandbennett.com
dan@mortimerandbennett.com
⊖ / ⇌ Turnham Green

OVERVIEW

First opened
1990
Owner
Dan Mortimer

CHEESE

No. available
75
Countries of origin
Britain, France, Ireland, Italy, Spain, Switzerland

PRICING per 100g

Brie de Meaux	£2.20
Mature Cheddar	£1.60 - £2.20
Parmigiano-Reggiano	£2.40
Stilton	£2.30

Mr Christian's Delicatessen

11 Elgin Crescent, W11 2JA

OPEN

Mon-Fri.	7:30am - 6:30pm
Sat.	7:30am - 6:00pm
Sun.	8:00am - 3:00pm

Mr Christian's Delicatessen has been a food haven for Notting Hill residents and visitors to Portobello Market for the past 40 years. The cheeses are mostly French and perfect to enjoy with the store's saucisson. Choose a suitable accompaniment from the extensive selection of homemade preserves decorating the shelves. The shop is owned by its neighbour, Jeroboams, so you can pop next door and pick up a bottle of wine to match your cheese selection.

CONTACT

020 7229 0501
www.mrchristians.co.uk
alex.oliveira@mrchristians.co.uk
⊖ / ≉ Ladbroke Grove

OVERVIEW

First opened
1974
Owner
The Jeroboams Group

CHEESE

No. available
50
Countries of origin
Britain, France, Ireland, Italy, Spain, Switzerland

PRICING per 100g

Brie de Meaux	£2.00
Mature Cheddar	£2.10
Parmigiano-Reggiano	£2.80
Stilton	£2.00

Raoul's Deli

8-10 Clifton Road, W9 1SS

OPEN

Mon-Fri.	7:30am - 8:30pm
Sat.	7:30am - 8:00pm
Sun.	8:30am - 7:00pm

Every mouth-watering item in Raoul's Deli is beautifully presented, from the vegetables outside to the cooked goods behind the counter. The shop sells a particularly good selection of goat's milk cheeses from Britain, France, Italy and Spain, amongst a broader range of traditional cheeses from these countries.

CONTACT

020 7289 6649
www.raoulsgourmet.com
headoffice@raoulsgourmet.com
⊖ / ⇄ Warwick Avenue

Other London locations
Hammersmith

OVERVIEW

First opened
1999
Owner
Geraldine Leventis

CHEESE

No. available
35
Countries of origin
Britain, France, Italy,
Netherlands, Spain

PRICING per 100g

Brie de Meaux	£2.50
Mature Cheddar	£2.45
Parmigiano-Reggiano	£3.20
Stilton	£2.35

Sourced Market

St. Pancras International, Pancras Road, NW1 2QP

OPEN

Mon-Fri.	7:00am - 9:00pm
Sat.	8:00am - 8:00pm
Sun.	10:00am - 8:00pm

A few years ago it would have been inconceivable to find quality food at a British railway station. But a visit to Sourced Market at St. Pancras (near the Thameslink entrance) will demonstrate how things have changed. The store sells locally-sourced, seasonal goods including charcuterie, fresh produce and delicatessen.
The cheese offering is varied, and the British selection impresses many a French Eurostar traveller. There is an interesting range of natural wines supplied by Les Caves de Pyrene as well as a handful of London-brewed beers.

CONTACT

020 7833 9352
www.sourcedmarket.com
info@sourcedmarket.com
 / ⇌ King's Cross / St. Pancras

Other London locations
Hildreth Street Market /
Venn Street Market

OVERVIEW

First opened
2009
Owner
Ben O'Brien

CHEESE

No. available
30
Countries of origin
Britain, France, Italy, Spain

PRICING per 100g

Brie de Meaux	£2.40
Mature Cheddar	£2.50
Parmigiano-Reggiano	£2.40
Stilton	£2.50

Terroni of Clerkenwell

138-140 Clerkenwell Road, EC1R 5DL

OPEN

Mon.	Closed
Tue.-Fri.	8:00am - 6:00pm
Sat.	9:00am - 5:00pm
Sun.	10:00am - 2:00pm

Terroni of Clerkenwell was founded in 1878, making it the oldest Italian deli in London. The shop's image recently received a revamp but the charming black and white photos on the walls recall the store in times gone by. As expected, all the cheeses are Italian and there is a particularly good selection of Pecorino. The Italian wines are smartly labelled, with detailed tasting notes to help you choose your favourite.

OVERVIEW

First opened
1878
Owner
The Andessa Family and Mr Sula

CONTACT

020 7837 1712
www.terroni.co.uk
info@terroni.co.uk
 / ⇌ Farringdon

CHEESE

No. available
25
Countries of origin
Italy

PRICING per 100g
Parmigiano-Reggiano   £2.50

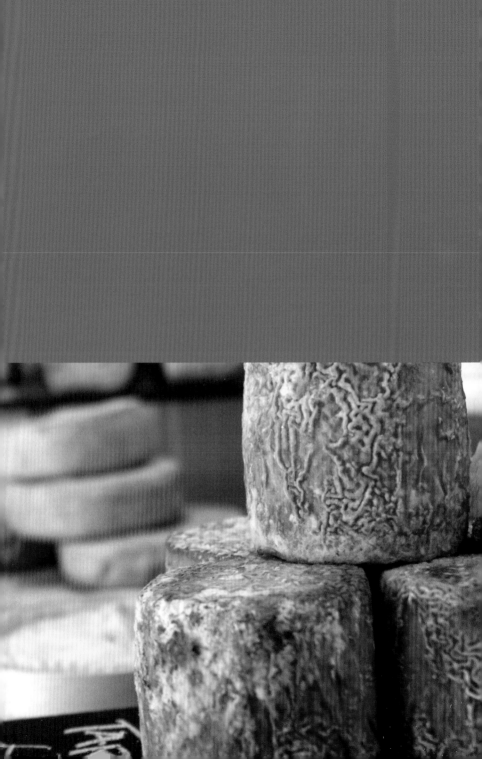

Markets

London's markets are thriving gastronomic venues selling an abundance of fresh food. Between Borough and Bermondsey you will find more cheese sellers than anywhere else in London but head to any farmers' market in the capital for some of Britain's best cheeses.

Borough Market

8 Southwark Street, SE1 1TL

CONTACT

020 7407 1002
www.boroughmarket.org.uk
info@boroughmarket.org.uk
⊖ / ⇌ London Bridge

Borough Market has existed since the 13th century and is London's oldest fruit and vegetable market. The market now sells an astonishing range of fresh produce as well as delicious cooked food from every corner of the world. With around 13 stalls selling cheese, it is a cheese lover's paradise. Some of the stalls are dedicated to one type of cheese such as Comté or Parmigiano-Reggiano. Other stalls sell a good range of British, French, Italian or Swiss cheeses. All the traders care passionately about cheese and are more than happy to share their knowledge. There is something for everyone at Borough Market and whilst you may have to battle the tourists on a Saturday, it is worth it for the fantastic and unique cheese experience.

Borough Market

Alsop & Walker

CONTACT
01825 831 810
www.alsopandwalker.co.uk
info@alsopandwalker.co.uk

Owner
Arthur Alsop and Nicholas Walker
Specialty
East Sussex artisan cheese

This East Sussex artisan cheesemaker produces a range of cheese, from soft to hard and smoked to blue. Our attention was drawn to Lord London – a brand new cheese that has already received acclaim. Not only was the cheese a silver award winner at the World Cheese Awards 2011 but it was also chosen by Will and Kate, Duke and Duchess of Cambridge, for their wedding breakfast.

Beillevaire

CONTACT
020 7584 1231
www.fromagerie-beillevaire.com
f.beillevaire@beillevaire.com

Owner
Fabrice Beillevaire
Specialty
French cheese

This is an off-shoot of the main Knightsbridge store, selling a small selection of Beillevaire's 400 cheeses alongside cream, butter and yoghurt made at the Beillevaire dairy. Try the family's homemade Machecoulais, an oval washed rind cheese produced in the Vendeen marshes with a rich and creamy texture and slightly lactic flavour.

Bianca e Mora

Owner
Emilia Ltd
Specialty
Parmigiano-Reggiano

Bianca e Mora specialises in produce from the Emilia-Romagna region of Italy, in particular charcuterie and Parmigiano-Reggiano. The Parmigiano is made from the milk of rare regional "vacche rosse" or red cows and matured for 24 to 36 months. This Parmigiano is creamier than most and matches perfectly with "saba" (a sweet reduction of grape must) or aged balsamic vinegar, both available at the stall.

CONTACT
www.biancaemora.com
info@emilialtd.co.uk

Borough Cheese Company

Owner
Jason Hinds and Dominic Coyte
Specialty
Comté

This stall only sells Comté, the most popular cheese in France. The Comté is matured by renowned affineur, Marcel Petite, and brought over by Borough Cheese Company from the Haut Doubs region every six weeks. Wheels aged for 15 months are stacked high on the market stall. Tasting is encouraged and you will walk away with a superbly produced, matured and well-cut piece of Comté.

CONTACT
www.boroughcheesecompany.co.uk
info@boroughcheesecompany.co.uk

The French Comté

Owner
Fabien Joly and Florent Gacon
Specialty
Comté

Best friends Fabien Joly and Florent Gacon started The French Comté together in early 2011 to bring the flavours of the French mountains to London. At this stall you can enjoy Comté aged for 12, 18, 24 and even 36 months. They also sell cheeses you will not find anywhere else in London including Le Cacouyard (an unpasteurised cow's milk cheese infused with walnuts) and L'Édel de Cléron (similar to Vacherin Mont d'Or and also wrapped in spruce bark with creamy, mushroomy flavours).

CONTACT
07543 384 859
www.thefrenchcomte.co.uk
fabien@thefrenchcomte.co.uk

Gastronomica

Owner
Marco Vineis
Specialty
Italian cheese

Gastronomica has been at Borough Market since 2000 and sells cheeses from all over Italy, Sicily and Sardinia, although Piedmont is its speciality region. Ask the stall manager, Joseph Tchikou, to talk you through the selection - he has the most extraordinary knowledge of his cheeses and is passionate about each one. You will be taken on a tour of Italian history, culture and terroir as Joseph explains the array of cheeses in front of you. This is a fantastic experience and the cheese is excellent.

CONTACT
020 7407 4488
www.gastronomica.co.uk
info@gastronomica.co.uk

Gorwydd Caerphilly

Owner
Trethowan's Dairy
Specialty
Gorwydd Caerphilly

Gorwydd Caephilly is made by Trethowan's Dairy in Ceredigion, Wales. It is produced in the traditional way using unpasteurised milk and animal rennet. This delicious cheese is matured for two months giving it a distinctive brown-grey rind and two-tone paste: yellow and creamy towards the rind, pale and crumbly in the centre. The rind has a mushroomy flavour, which is well-balanced by the fresh lemony interior.

CONTACT
01179 020 332
www.trethowansdairy.co.uk
info@trethowansdairy.co.uk

Jumi

Owner
Juerg and Mike
Specialty
Swiss cheese

This stall is the place to go for top quality Swiss cheese, almost all of which is made by family and friends of the owners. Be sure to try their Cironé, a complex and sophisticated hard cow's milk cheese matured for two years, and Belper Knolle (pronounced Can-o-le), a small rock-hard cheese infused with Himalayan salt and local garlic then rubbed in black pepper – the intense flavour makes it perfect for shaving over pasta, salad or soup.

CONTACT
www.jumi.lu
london@jumi.lu

Kappacasein

Owner
Bill Oglethorpe
Specialty
Ogleshield raclette and Montgomery's Cheddar toasted sandwiches

At Kappacasein, Bill Oglethorpe serves up melted Ogleshield raclette, oozing over crushed new potatoes, accompanied by gherkins and grilled Bermondsey Frier (like halloumi but oh-so-much better!). Also on offer are glorious grilled cheese sandwiches made with Montgomery's Cheddar, Poilâne sourdough, onions, leeks and garlic. Bill is also London's only professional cheesemaker. Try Bermondsey Frier, Bermondsey Hard Press and Spa Lactic, all produced at his dairy under the London Bridge railway arches.

CONTACT
www.kappacasein.com
bill@kappacasein.com

L'Ubriaco - Drunk Cheese

Owner
Pam Melotti and Max Secci
Specialty
Ubriaco cheese

Ubriaco is cheese from Veneto in Italy, which has been soaked in grape must during the maturing process. This gives the cheese a sweet winey flavour and moist texture. The stall sells five different types of Ubriaco including a goat and cow's milk cheese that has been matured for one year in Barolo wine, a blue sheep's cheese matured in the sweet wine Passito di Pantelleria and a cow's milk cheese matured in Prosecco.

CONTACT
07947 246 517
info.ubriaco@yahoo.co.uk

Mons Cheesemongers

Owner
Hervé Mons
Specialty
French cheese

Mons, an established French fromager and affineur, came to London in 2006. The stall sells a small selection of well-chosen French and Swiss cheeses, some of which are matured in France and others in the newly constructed maturing rooms under the London Bridge railway arches. You will spot familiar favourites, like Langres and Saint-Marcellin, and discover some rarer seasonal cheeses. We recommend this stall to any cheese aficionado.

CONTACT
020 7064 6912
www.mons-cheese.co.uk
info@mons-cheese.co.uk

The Parmesan Cheese Company

Owner
Alison Elliott and Elliott John
Specialty
Parmigiano-Reggiano

The Parmigiano at this stall is made in the foothills of the Parma Apennines, by one dairy which produces just four wheels of cheese each day from a small herd of Swiss Brown cows. The Parmesan Cheese Company's sister business, The Ham & Cheese Co., can be found at Spa Road where it sells buffalo Mozzarella and a splendid selection of Continental charcuterie as well as Parmigiano.

CONTACT
07970 532 485
www.thehamandcheeseco.co.uk
info@thehamandcheeseco.com

Une Normande à Londres

Owner
Franck, Yann and Cedric Leblais
Specialty
French cheese

This stall sells a large range of French cheeses, which are sourced each week from France by brothers Franck, Yann and Cedric Leblais. One of their more unusual cheeses is "Franglais" – a traditional Camembert soaked in New Forest Cider and then rolled in breadcrumbs at the company's base in Vauxhall.

CONTACT
020 8607 9762
www.unenormandealondres.co.uk
normandealondres@yahoo.fr

LONDON MARKET CHEESE STALLS

LONDON MARKET \ CHEESE TRADER	Alham Wood Cheeses	Alsop & Walker	Batch Farm Cheeses	The Bath Soft Cheese Co.	Beillevaire	Bianca e Mora	Boerenkaas	Borough Cheese Company	Brinkworth Dairy and Ceri's Cheese	The Dark Knights of Cholesterol	Ellie's Dairy	Fielding Cottage	The French Comté	Gastronomica	Gorwydd Caerphilly	Greenfields of…
Alexandra Palace				2, 4												
Archway	E															
Balham				1					E		2	4				2
Blackheath	E		2, 3, 4, 5			E										
Bloomsbury				1, 3												2
Borough		E			E	E		E					E	E	E Fri-Sat.	
Brixton Village	E		4	1, 3, 5												1, 2
Broadgate				2, 4												
Broadway (Hackney)																
Chatsworth Road										E						
Ealing	E			1												1, 2
East Dulwich																
Hackney Homemade										E						
Hammersmith				1, 3												
Hildreth Street														E		
Islington	E		2, 5	2, 4												1
Lower Marsh										E Fri. only						
Marylebone	E			1, 3, 5					2							2
Notting Hill	E			3								2, 4				2
Oval				2, 4												
Parliament Hill	E		1	2, 4												3
Parsons Green				2, 4							1					1, 3
Partridges						E		E								
Pimlico	E		2, 5	4												
Real Food								E								
Queens Park	1, 2, 4, 5		1, 3, 5					E								3
South Kensington				3, 5								1				
Spa Road							E Druid St									
Stoke Newington	E			E												
Swiss Cottage	E			E												
Tachbrook Street										E Fri-Sat.				E		
Twickenham	E		1, 3, 5	2, 4								2, 5				
Venn Street						E								E		
Walthamstow	E		2													1, 3
West Hampstead			2, 4	1, 3, 5					E		3	1, 5				
Wimbledon	E		2, 4, 5	1, 5							4	3				1

Hurdlebrook Dairy	Jumi	Kappacasein	KäseSwiss	Lincolnshire Poacher	L'Ubriaco	Mons Cheesemongers	Moqtown	Neal's Yard Dairy	Norbiton Fine Cheese Co	Nut Knowle Farm	The Parmesan Cheese Company	Sourced Market	Une Normande à Londres	White Lake Cheese	Windrush Valley Goat Dairy	Wobbly Bottom Farm
									E	E						
										1						
										2, 3, 4, 5				1		
	E	E			E	E						E	E			
									E							
				4						3, 5						
							E Sat. only									
												E	E			
1, 3				5						1, 3, 5			E		4	2
1, 3				5						1, 3, 5			E		2, 4	4
E				4						1, 3, 5						
								E								
										1, 2, 3, 5						4
										2, 4				3		
	E												E			
				4						1, 3, 5					2, 4	
				5						1, 3, 5				2, 4	2	4
										3, 4, 5					2	
	E Ness St	E Druid St				E Ness St		E Ness St								

KEY

E	every week
1	first week of the month
2	second week of the month
3	third week of the month
4	fourth week of the month
5	fifth week of the month

Traders may take a week off or change their market schedule. If you wish to visit a particular trader, then it is best to contact them in advance

Hurdlebrook Dairy	Jumi	Kappacasein	KäseSwiss	Lincolnshire Poacher	L'Ubriaco	Mons Cheesemongers	Moqtown	Neal's Yard Dairy	Norbiton Fine Cheese Co	Nut Knowle Farm	The Parmesan Cheese Company	Sourced Market	Une Normande à Londres	White Lake Cheese	Windrush Valley Goat Dairy	Wobbly Bottom Farm
										4, 5						
												E				
										2					4	
										2, 5						

LONDON MARKET DIRECTORY

MARKET	ADDRESS	POST CODE	⊖ / ≹	TRADING HOURS
Alexandra Palace	Alexandra Palace Park (Muswell Hill Entrance)	N10 3TG	Alexandra Palace / Wood Green	**Sun.** 10:00am - 3:00pm
Archway	Holloway Road	N19 5SS	Archway / Upper Holloway	**Sat.** 10:00am - 5:00pm
Balham	Chestnut Grove Primary School, Chestnut Grove / Hearnville Road	SW12 8JZ	Balham	**Sat.** 9:00am - 2:00pm
Blackheath	Blackheath Station Car Park	SE3 9LA	Blackheath	**Sun.** 10:00am - 2:00pm
Bloomsbury	Torrington Square / Byng Place	WC1E 7HY	Goodge Street / Euston Square	**Thu.** 9:00am - 2:00pm
Borough	8 Southwark Street	SE1 1TL	London Bridge	Open just for lunch **Mon-Wed.** 10:00am - 3:00pm Full market **Thu.** 11:00am - 5:00pm **Fri.** 12:00pm - 6:00pm **Sat.** 8:00am - 5:00pm
Brixton Village	Brixton Station Road	SW9 8PA	Brixton	**Sun.** 10:00am - 2:00pm
Broadgate	Finsbury Avenue Square	EC2M 2QS	Liverpool Street	**Thu.** 8:00am - 2:00pm (Weeks 2 and 4 only)
Broadway (Hackney)	London Fields to Regent's Canal	E8 4QB	London Fields	**Sat.** 9:00am - 5:00pm
Chatsworth Road	Chatsworth Road	E5 0LH	Homerton	**Sun.** 11:00am - 4:00pm
Ealing	Leeland Road	W13 9HH	West Ealing	**Sat.** 9:00am - 1:00pm
East Dulwich	North Cross Road	SE22 9EV	East Dulwich	**Fri-Sat.** 9:00am - 5:00pm
Hackney Homemade	St John's Church Gardens	E5 0PD	Hackney Central	**Sat.** 11:00am - 4:00pm
Hammersmith	Lyric Square	W6 0QL	Hammersmith	**Thu.** 10:00am - 3:00pm
Hildreth Street	Hildreth Street	SW12 9RQ	Balham	**Sun.** 10:00am - 4:00pm
Islington	Chapel Market, Penton Street / Baron Street	N1 9PZ	Angel	**Sun.** 10:00am - 2:00pm
Lower Marsh	Lower Marsh	SE1 7AB	Waterloo	**Mon-Fri.** 10:00am - 4:00pm
Marylebone	Cramer Street Car Park	W1U 4EW	Baker Street	**Sun.** 10:00am - 2:00pm

MARKET	ADDRESS	POST CODE	⊖ / ⇌	TRADING HOURS
Notting Hill	Car Park behind Waterstones, Kensington Church Street	W11 3PB	Notting Hill Gate	**Sat.** 9:00am - 1:00pm
Oval	St Mark's Church, The Oval	SE11 4PW	Oval	**Sat.** 10:00am - 3:00pm
Parliament Hill	William Ellis School, Highgate Road	NW5 1RN	Gospel Oak	**Sat.** 10:00am - 2:00pm
Parsons Green	New Kings School, New King's Road	SW6 4LY	Parsons Green / Putney Bridge	**Sun.** 10:00am - 2:00pm
Partridges	Duke of York Square	SW3 4LY	Sloane Square	**Sat.** 10:00am - 4:00pm
Pimlico	Pimlico Road / Ebury Street	SW1W 8UT	Sloane Square	**Sat.** 9:00am - 1:00pm
Real Food	Southbank Centre	SE1 8XX	Waterloo	**Fri.** 12:00pm - 8:00pm **Sat.** 11:00am - 8:00pm **Sun.** 12:00pm - 6:00pm
Queens Park	Salusbury Primary School, Salusbury Road	NW6 6RG	Brondesbury Park	**Sun.** 10:00am - 2:00pm
South Kensington	Bute Street	SW7 3EX	South Kensington	**Sat.** 9:00am - 2:00pm
Spa Road	Druid Street / Dockley Road / Voyager Business Park (Ness Street)	SE1 / SE16	Bermondsey	**Sat.** 9:00am - 2:00pm
Stoke Newington	St Paul's Church, Stoke Newington High Street	N16 7UY	Rectory Road	**Sat.** 10:00am - 2:30pm
Swiss Cottage	Eton Avenue	NW3 3EU	Swiss Cottage	**Wed.** 10:00am - 3:00pm
Tachbrook Street	Tachbrook Street	SW1V 2JS	Victoria / Pimlico	**Mon-Sat.** 10:00am - 4:00pm
Twickenham	Holly Road Car Park	TW1 4HF	Twickenham	**Sat.** 9:00am - 1:00pm
Venn Street	Venn Street	SW4 0AT	Clapham Common	**Sat.** 10:00am - 4:00pm
Walthamstow	The Town Square, Selbourne Walk / the High Street	E17 7JN	Walthamstow Central	**Sun.** 10:00am - 2:00pm
West Hampstead	West Hampstead Thameslink Station, Iverson Road	NW6 1PF	West Hampstead Thameslink	**Sat.** 10:00am - 2:00pm
Wimbledon	Wimbledon Park Primary School, Havana Road	SW19 8EJ	Wimbledon Park	**Sat.** 9:00am - 1:00pm

Alham Wood Cheeses

CONTACT

01749 880 221
www.buffalo-organics.co.uk
alhamwood@supanet.com

Owner
Frances Wood
Specialty
Buffalo's milk cheese

This is the place to come for organic buffalo cheese (as well as steak and yoghurt). Alham Wood sells seven different buffalo cheeses, all made using milk from the farm's buffalo in Somerset. There are some great soft cheeses, including Mozzarella, but be sure to try Alham Wood's famed hard cheese, Junas, named after the matriarch of the herd.

The Bath Soft Cheese Co.

Image supplied by The Bath Soft Cheese Co.

CONTACT

01225 331 601
www.parkfarm.co.uk
sales@parkfarm.co.uk

Owner
The Padfield Family
Specialty
Bath Soft Cheese

Run by the Padfield family, The Bath Soft Cheese Co. makes Bath Soft Cheese in Somerset using a traditional recipe dating back hundreds of years. This cheese has earned the company a reputation for being one of the finest artisan cheesemakers in Britain.

Boerenkaas

Owner
Rachael Sills
Specialty
Dutch farmhouse cheese

Boerenkaas sells some of the best Dutch farmhouse cheese in London, including aged Gouda and the incredible award-winning Olde Remeker. Boerenkaas and its sister company, KäseSwiss, intend to move from their current location on Druid Street to Spa Road within the next year or so.

CONTACT
07783 542 310
www.dutchfarmhousecheese.co.uk
dutchcheese@kaseswiss.co.uk

The Dark Knights of Cholesterol

Owner
Ian Willingham and
Gianalberto Kiefner
Specialty
English and Italian cheese

Ian and Gianalberto sell fantastic cheeses from across Europe and can talk you through the background to each one. They have a particularly good selection from Piedmont and Lombardy as well as traditional cheeses from Cheshire specialist, H.S. Bourne.

KäseSwiss

CONTACT
07783 542 310
www.kaseswiss.com
rachael@kaseswiss.co.uk

Owner
Rachael Sills
Specialty
Swiss cheese

Located on Druid Street next to its sister company, Boerenkaas, KäseSwiss sells around ten beautiful Swiss mountain cheeses, including Heublumen (which is coated in sweet hay from the hills of St. Gallen) and Tomme Fleurette (soft and milky, and the youngest Swiss cheese sold in the UK) as well as the more familiar Gruyère and Emmental.

Mootown

CONTACT
07974 099 035
www.mootown.co.uk
cheese@mootown.co.uk

Owner
Tom Harding
Specialty
Welsh cheese

Mootown's selection of Welsh farmhouse cheese includes Golden Cenarth, Teifi, Gorwydd Caerphilly and Perl Las. Look out for the stall's speciality cheese, Bermondsey Spa, which is a Golden Cenarth washed in Kernel Brewery pale ale and matured in a wooden box that is perfect for baking.

Norbiton Fine Cheese Co

Owner
Bryan Barrington
Specialty
British and Irish cheese

Norbiton Fine Cheese Co is primarily a wholesale business and has an excellent British and Irish artisan cheese selection. The company's ethos is for each stall to feel like a village shop so it will not be long before the enthusiastic traders know your name and favourite cheeses. They also stock a small selection of European cheeses.

CONTACT
020 8605 2412
www.norbitoncheese.co.uk
info@norbitoncheese.co.uk

Nut Knowle Farm

Image supplied by Nut Knowle Farm

Owner
Lyn and Jenny Jenner
Specialty
Goat's milk cheese

Nut Knowle Farm in Sussex makes 15 different goat's cheeses with milk from the farm's Toggenburg and British Saanen goats. The range is varied and includes the hard Sussex Yeoman, the soft and charcoal-covered Wealdway Mature and the crottin-style Wealden.

CONTACT
www.nutknowlefarm.com
jj@nutknowlefarm.com

Veneto

Wine

BOTTLE CLOSURE

A wine bottle is stoppered by a cork (natural or synthetic) or a screw cap. Natural cork is the traditional material used to seal a bottle but screw caps and synthetic corks are becoming increasingly popular and should not be seen as a mark of low quality.

BOTTLE SHAPE

The shape of a wine bottle differs depending on region and type of wine. Bordeaux bottles have a straight neck and sides and tall shoulders. Burgundy bottles have sloping shoulders and a slightly wider middle. An Alsace bottle is easily recognisable by its tall and fluted shape. Champagne bottles are made of thicker glass and have a wide punt (the indentation at the base of the bottle) to withstand the build up of pressure caused by the bubbles.

NAME OF THE WINE PRODUCER

This is the name of the estate or organisation that made the wine. It is often the most prominent name on the label and is a general indicator of quality.

BOTTLE SIZE

Until the mid-twentieth century, wine bottles ranged in size between 500ml and 800ml depending on the region. Wine bottles did not become the standard 750ml until 1979, when the US moved to the Metric system and required all US wine bottles to convert to this size from the American "fifth". The European Union followed suit to facilitate the process of standardisation.

A Wine Bottle Explained

VINTAGE

The vintage is the year the grapes were grown and harvested and can be an important indicator of the wine's quality. By knowing the vintage you can also calculate whether the wine is ready for drinking. Some wines, particularly New World wines, can be enjoyed immediately after bottling whereas others should be kept for a few years (or decades) before they will taste their best.

ALCOHOL CONTENT

Old World wines usually have an alcohol content of 11% to 13.5%. New World wines tend to have a higher alcohol content, often between 13% and 15%, a result of riper grapes in these regions, linked to higher levels of sunshine.

WINE REGION

The place where the grapes were grown. A wine's region plays an important part in determining taste. "Terroir", the essence of a given region, imparts distinctive flavour and aroma to a wine. Two wines made with grapes of the same variety but in different regions can taste dramatically different.

NAME OF THE WINE

Many wines are given the same name as the grape variety from which the wine is made. Other wines are named after the region where the grapes were grown, for example Chianti or Burgundy. Wines can also be given more creative names. Many wine names involve animals and others tie in with the history of the winery. Some winemakers name their wines with a light-hearted pun, such as "Goats do Roam" - a play on Côtes du Rhône.

GRAPE VARIETY

If the label states one particular grape variety, in this example Cabernet Franc, then the wine must comprise at least 85% of that variety. Otherwise, the wine will be described as a "blend". Many regional wines are blended, such as Bordeaux and Rioja.

Wine Merchants

There is a real choice of style when it comes to London's wine merchants. Discuss your requirements and purchase on recommendation or opt for enomatic sampling and "try before you buy". Whether you are buying table wine or fine vintages, you never need to compromise on quality and individuality.

259 Hackney Road

259 Hackney Road, E2 8NA

ORGANIC

The entire stock of this small, quirky shop sits on a wooden table and a couple of shelves. This is the place to come for natural French wine and the 40 or so bottles sold here are exclusive in London to this shop, brought over by the owners. A painted white number on each display bottle indicates price. 259 Hackney Road is simple and charming, and definitely worth a visit if you are after something bespoke with a story to match.

OPEN

Mon.	Closed
Tue-Sat.	11:00am - 9:00pm
Sun.	11:00am - 6:00pm

OVERVIEW

First opened
February 2012
Owner
Florian Tonello and Milena Bucholz

....

WINE

No. available
40
Specialty
Natural French wine

PRICING

Per bottle	£8 - £90
Av. bottle sold	£15

....

CONTACT

07596 838 373
www.259hackneyroad.com
info@259hackneyroad.com
⊖ / ⇌ Hoxton

Wine Merchants

Berry Bros. & Rudd

3 St James's Street, SW1A 1EG

Most wine merchants consider Berry Bros. & Rudd to be the best in the country, if not the world, and this flagship store is an essential destination for any oenophile. Berry Bros. & Rudd has been at No. 3 St James's Street since its opening in 1698 and the iconic black and gold façade is an established part of the London landscape. The fascinating interior records 300 years of English history and could distract you for hours. Only a small proportion of stock is on display so engage the expertise of a smartly attired assistant. Take home one of the Berry Bros. & Rudd own blends as a special souvenir of your visit.

71

Images supplied by Berry Bros. & Rudd

OPEN

Mon-Fri.	10:00am - 6:00pm
Sat.	10:00am - 5:00pm
Sun.	Closed

OVERVIEW

First opened
1698
Owner
The Berry and Rudd Families

....

WINE

No. available
1,000
Specialty
Old World wine

PRICING

Per bottle	£7 - £14,250
Av. bottle sold	£18

....

CONTACT

0800 280 2440
www.bbr.com
bbr@bbr.com
⊖ / ⇌ Green Park

Bottle Apostle

95 Lauriston Road, E9 7HJ

OPEN

Mon.	Closed
Tue-Fri.	12:00pm - 9:00pm
Sat.	10:00am - 8:00pm
Sun.	10:00am - 6:00pm

Bottle Apostle is one of the many fantastic independent shops in Victoria Park, giving the area a country village feel despite the East End location. This shop appeals to wine novices and experts alike, with a diverse collection of wines and genuine range of prices. Colour-coded wine labels are user-friendly and include suggested food pairings. There are always 32 wines to taste and knowledgeable members of staff on hand to help.

CONTACT

020 8985 1549
www.bottleapostle.com
info@bottleapostle.com
⊖ / ⇌ London Fields

Other London locations
Crouch End

OVERVIEW

First opened
2009
Owner
Andrew Eakin

WINE

No. available
350 - 400
No. to sample
32
Specialty
Austrian and Portuguese wine

PRICING

Per sample	£0.50 - £6
Per bottle	£7 - £380
Av. bottle sold	£15

City Beverage Company

303 Old Street, EC1V 9IA

OPEN

Mon-Thu.	10:00am - 9:30pm
Fri.	10:00am - 10:00pm
Sat.	10:30am - 10:30pm
Sun.	10:30am - 7:30pm

Referred to by regulars as "The Old Curiosity Shop", this unique store was enticing visitors to Shoreditch long before it became one of London's trendiest areas. Alongside the selection of wines sit tea leaves, coffee beans and seven locally-brewed beers. Look out for the famous drinking quotes dotted around the store to boost your wine trivia knowledge.

CONTACT

020 7729 2111
www.citybeverage.co.uk
info@citybeverage.co.uk
 / Old Street

OVERVIEW

First opened
1982
Owner
Stuart Edwards and Brian Towe

WINE

No. available
900
Specialty
French wine

PRICING

Per bottle	£5 - £1,000
Av. bottle sold	£9.50

Green & Blue Wines

38 Lordship Lane, SE22 8HJ

OPEN

Mon-Wed.	11:00am - 11:00pm
Thu-Fri.	11:00am - midnight
Sat.	10:00am - midnight
Sun.	12:00pm - 5:00pm

Green & Blue Wines is an easy-going wine shop and bar, based on an Italian enoteca. The shop is a great location to discover some lesser-known wines, which are arranged by style rather than region to help the inexperienced wine buyer. To assist further, each label has a suggested food pairing. A couple of bottles are usually open for tasting or you can try a glass at the bar before making your decision.

CONTACT

020 8693 9250
www.greenandbluewines.com
info@greenandbluewines.com
⊖ / ⇄ East Dulwich

OVERVIEW

First opened
2005
Owner
Kate Thal

WINE

No. available
285
Specialty
Organic, biodynamic and natural wine

PRICING

Per bottle	£7.50 - £180
Av. bottle sold	£11

Handford Wines

105 Old Brompton Road, SW7 3LE

OPEN

Mon-Sat.	10:00am - 8:30pm
Sun.	11:00am - 5:00pm

Handford Wines is a traditional merchant with a loyal customer base, many of whom have shopped here for over two decades and would not dream of going anywhere else. It is one of the only small UK wine merchants to boast two Masters of Wine, owner James Handford and senior buyer Greg Sherwood, who have filled the shop to the rafters with fine wines from around the world and are more than happy to share their expertise.

CONTACT

020 7589 6113
www.handford.net
mick@handford.net
⊖ / ⇌ South Kensington

OVERVIEW

First opened
1989
Owner
James Handford

WINE

No. available
2,000
Specialty
Bordeaux and Burgundy

PRICING

Per bottle	£8 - £2,000
Av. bottle sold	£15

Haynes Hanson & Clark

7 Elystan Street, SW3 3NT

OPEN

Mon-Fri.	9:00am - 7:00pm
Sat.	9:00am - 4:30pm
Sun.	Closed

Haynes Hanson & Clark enthusiastically describe themselves as "a place to buy jolly good wine", adding "there's not much more to it than that". And perhaps this no-nonsense approach is why they have remained one of London's most respected merchants after 35 years in the business. The shop is located on Chelsea Green; an idyllic village in the centre of London, with superb independent food shops and just a hair's breadth away from the King's Road.

CONTACT

020 7584 7927
www.hhandc.co.uk
london@hhandc.co.uk
⊖ / ⮀ South Kensington

OVERVIEW

First opened
1978
Owner
Nicholas Clark

WINE

No. available
380
Specialty
Burgundy

PRICING

Per bottle	£5.50 - £3,000
Av. bottle sold	£13.50

Jeroboams

50-52 Elizabeth Street, SW1W 9PB

OPEN

Mon-Fri.	9:30am - 7:00pm
Sat.	10:00am - 5:00pm
Sun.	Closed

Following Jeroboams' steady expansion over the past 15 years, it is now London's largest independent wine merchant and has seven stores located in some of the smartest areas. It specialises in fine wine and Champagne but the comprehensive international offering includes wine from the New World, Central Europe and the Middle East. The Holland Park store was originally established as a cheese shop and still has a tempting cheese selection along with charcuterie and other fine foods.

CONTACT

020 7730 8108
www.jeroboams.co.uk
granville.murray@jeroboams.co.uk
⊖ / ⇌ Victoria

Other London locations
Hampstead / Holland Park / Knightsbridge / Mayfair / Milroy's of Soho / Notting Hill

OVERVIEW

First opened
1988
Owner
Peter Rich

WINE

No. available
1,000
No. to sample
8
Specialty
Bordeaux

PRICING

Per sample	From £0.50
Per bottle	£4 - £10,000
Av. bottle sold	£15

Lea & Sandeman

170 Fulham Road, SW10 9PR

OPEN

Mon-Sat.	10:00am - 8:00pm
Sun.	Closed

Lea & Sandeman was one of the first merchants to bring wine to the London high street. At this highly respected establishment, you will buy first class wine and receive excellent advice. The aim of the shop's owners is to sell wine with personality for enjoyable drinking, rather than focusing on big-name labels. In the bright and airy flagship store, there is a great selection of bottles for immediate drinking as well as for laying down.

CONTACT

020 7244 0522
www.leaandsandeman.co.uk
david@leaandsandeman.co.uk
⊖ / ⇌ South Kensington

Other London locations
Barnes / Chiswick / Kensington

OVERVIEW

First opened
1988
Owner
Charles Lea and Patrick Sandeman

....

WINE

No. available
1,000
Specialty
French and Italian wine

PRICING

Per bottle	£6 - £800
Av. bottle sold	£10

....

Majestic

21a-23 Loudoun Road, NW8 0ND

OPEN

Mon-Fri.	10:00am - 8:00pm
Sat.	9:00am - 7:00pm
Sun.	10:00am - 5:00pm

Majestic is a household name on the high street, known for branded wine at affordable prices. The key feature of this flagship store is an impressive Fine Wine Centre with big name vintages from the Old World and quality wines from smaller vineyards in the New World. Majestic has a half case minimum purchase but, with fine wines from £20 and many bottles at significantly reduced prices, there are plenty of excellent value options.

CONTACT

020 7604 3461
www.majestic.co.uk
sjw@majestic.co.uk
⊖ / ⇌ St. John's Wood

Other London locations
45 London stores

OVERVIEW

First opened
2003
Owner
Majestic Wine PLC

WINE

No. available
700
No. to sample
7

PRICING

Per sample	Free
Per bottle	£5 - £1,600
Av. bottle sold	£16

Philglas & Swiggot

21 Northcote Road, SW11 1NG

OPEN

Mon-Fri.	11:00am - 7:00pm
Sat.	10:00am - 6:00pm
Sun.	12:00pm - 5:00pm

Philglas & Swiggot is a laid-back, friendly place that does not take itself too seriously (note the name of the shop). Even so, the focus is on high quality, interesting wines and personal service. The Australian selection is particularly strong and includes a couple of wines made in Victoria especially for the shop's owners, Mike and Karen Rogers. The French and Italian range is also impressive, with an emphasis on smaller producers.

CONTACT

020 7924 4494
www.philglas-swiggot.com
karen@philglas-swiggot.co.uk
⊖ / ≷ Clapham Junction

Other London locations
Marylebone / Richmond

OVERVIEW

First opened
1991
Owner
Karen and Mike Rogers

....

WINE

No. available
800

PRICING

Per bottle	£7 - £780
Av. bottle sold	£18

....

Planet of the Grapes

74-82 Queen Elizabeth Street, EC4N 4SJ

OPEN

Mon-Fri.	10:00am - midnight
Sat-Sun.	Closed

Planet of the Grapes now has three shops and an ever-growing fan base across London. The enthusiastic and knowledgeable team usually has a few bottles open for tasting to help you choose from the splendid and varied selection. Take any bottle to the bar for a £10 corkage fee and continue your education with the shop's wine books, available for browsing.

CONTACT

020 7248 1892
www.planetofthegrapes.co.uk
bowlane@planetofthegrapes.co.uk
 Mansion House

Other London locations
Leadenhall Market / New Oxford Street

OVERVIEW

First opened
2009
Owner
Marc Wise and Matt Harris

....

WINE

No. available
350
Specialty
Italian wine and Burgundy

PRICING

Per bottle	£8 - £1,850
Av. bottle sold	£15 - £20

....

Wine Merchants

Wine Merchants

Roberson Wine

348 Kensington High Street, W14 8NS

OPEN

Mon-Sat.   10:00am - 8:00pm
Sun.   12:00pm - 6:00pm

Roberson Wine is a sophisticated merchant, offering excellent wine and down-to-earth advice. Seasoned wine drinkers will take delight in a fine and rare selection dating back to 1900, with a particularly strong Bordeaux and Burgundy offering. There are also 150 wines for under £10 to encourage customers to develop their palates at home. Tasting days at the store provide engaging and informative education for wine enthusiasts of all levels.

CONTACT

020 7371 2121
www.robersonwine.com
enquiries@robersonwine.com
 / ⇌ Kensington Olympia

OVERVIEW
First opened
1991
Owner
Cliff Roberson

WINE
No. available
1,500
Specialty
French wine

PRICING
Per bottle   £5 - £7,500
Av. bottle sold £15

The Sampler

35 Thurloe Place, SW7 2HP

Wine Merchants

OPEN

| Mon-Sat. | 11:30am - 10:00pm |
| Sun. | 11:30am - 7:00pm |

Tasting is the name of the game here, with an ever-changing selection of 80 wines available to try. The bottles for tasting are arranged by grape variety, available in three different sized measures and include the world's finest vintages as well as wine for everyday drinking. For a £7.50 corkage fee you can choose any bottle to drink in the cosy downstairs wine bar, surrounded by some of the shop's oldest vintages, with the optional extra of a cheese or charcuterie platter.

CONTACT

020 7225 5091
www.thesampler.co.uk
jamie@thesampler.co.uk
⊖ / ⇌ South Kensington

Other London locations
Islington

OVERVIEW

First opened
2006
Owner
Jamie Hutchinson and Dawn Mannis

....

WINE

No. available
1,500
No. to sample
80
Specialty
Grower Champagne

PRICING

Per sample	£0.35 - £79
Per bottle	£6 - £2,100
Av. bottle sold	£20

....

Theatre of Wine

75 Trafalgar Road, SE10 9TS

Theatre of Wine certainly delivers a sense of theatricality, from the stage curtains adorning the entrance to the props displayed amongst the wine shelves. But this is no smoke and mirrors: the owners of Theatre of Wine are skilled at sourcing and you will remember your purchases as much as the shop's decoration. It is one of the only shops in London to specialise in Eastern European wines so experiment with something new and learn the story of the vineyard behind your bottle.

OPEN
Mon-Sat.   10:00am - 9:00pm
Sun.   12:00pm - 6:00pm

OVERVIEW
First opened
2002
Owner
Daniel Illsley and Jon Jackson

CONTACT
020 8858 6363
www.theatreofwine.com
greenwich@theatreofwine.com
⊖ / ⇌ Maze Hill

Other London locations
Tufnell Park

WINE
No. available
900
Specialty
Eastern European wine

PRICING
Per bottle   £6 - £360
Av. bottle sold   £10 - £15

Uncorked

Exchange Arcade, Broadgate, EC2M 3WA

OPEN

Mon-Fri	10:00am - 7:00pm
Sat-Sun.	Closed

Hidden amongst the banks of Bishopsgate, Uncorked is a treasure worth finding. It is a small but well stocked shop selling the best of the Old World with a focus on France. Uncorked admits that much of its wine is expensive, and that is no wonder given the location. But come in with a modest budget and you will still receive time and attention from staff including the wonderful "Wine Educator", Colin Wills. If you cannot decide then try the staff selection, a mixed case chosen by the shop and delivered to your door.

CONTACT

020 7638 5998
www.uncorked.co.uk
drink@uncorked.co.uk
⊖ / ≥ Liverpool Street

OVERVIEW

First opened
1994
Owner
Andrew Rae and Jim Griffen

WINE

No. available
1,500
Specialty
French wine

PRICING

Per bottle	£7 - £780
Av. bottle sold	£15

Vagabond Wines

18-22 Vanston Place, SW6 1AX

OPEN

Mon-Fri.	12:00pm - 9:00pm
Sat.	11:00am - 9:00pm
Sun.	11:00am - 8:00pm

It is super simple to choose a bottle at Vagabond because so many of the wines are available for tasting.
The wines are organised according to flavour, rather than by region, and each comes with tasting notes to take home. Open and light with high communal tables and a relaxed atmosphere, the shop is designed for customers to taste, share and discuss wine. This is an ideal venue for a novice to start learning about wine.

CONTACT

020 7381 1717
www.vagabondwines.co.uk
info@vagabondwines.co.uk
⊖ / ⇌ Fulham Broadway

OVERVIEW

First opened
2010
Owner
Stephen Finch

WINE

No. available
150
No. to sample
100
Specialty
Enomatic sampling

PRICING

Per sample	£0.55 - £4.50
Per bottle	£7 - £120
Av. bottle sold	£14

Vini Italiani

72 Old Brompton Road, SW7 3LQ

OPEN

Mon-Fri & Sun. 12:00pm - 8:00pm
Sat. 10:00am - 9:00pm

This sleek, chic and meticulously designed store is dedicated to the promotion of Italian wine in London through education and experience. The owners of Vini Italiani place high emphasis on events, courses and tastings to showcase their unrivalled collection of exclusively Italian wines representing all 20 regions of the country. An abundance of Italian passion and award-winning sommeliers make this one of London's top destinations for a taste of la dolce vita.

CONTACT

020 7225 2283
www.vini-italiani.co.uk
info@vini-italiani.co.uk
⊖ / ⇌ South Kensington

OVERVIEW

First opened
2011
Owner
Bruno Cernecca, Diuska Luppi and Matteo Berlucchi

....

WINE

No. available
530
No. to sample
16
Specialty
Italian wine

PRICING

Per sample	£0.40 - £2.50
Per bottle	£9.50 - £945
Av. bottle sold	£29

....

The Wine Tasting Shop

18 Hildreth Street, SW12 9RQ

OPEN

Mon-Sat.	11:00am - 9:00pm
Sun.	12:00pm - 5:00pm

The bright Scandinavian design of this shop lifts your spirits, as does the enthusiasm of owner Julia Michael. Julia believes in a non-interventionist approach to winemaking and selects her wines from the smallest producers who share her ethos.

The shop's mantra of "try before you buy" means there are always around 20 wines to taste in store as well as interactive tasting events for every level of wine drinker.

CONTACT

020 8616 8658

www.thewinetastingshop.co.uk

⊖ / ⇌ Balham

OVERVIEW

First opened
2011

Owner
Julia Michael

....

WINE

No. available
350

No. to sample
15 - 20

Specialty
Grower Champagne

PRICING

Per sample	From £0.50
Per bottle	£6.50 - £130
Av. bottle sold	£11

....

The Winery

4 Clifton Road, W9 1SS

OPEN

Mon-Sat.	11:00am - 9:30pm
Sun.	12:00pm - 8:00pm

Owner David Motion loves dry Riesling and you will too after a trip to The Winery. This store is the largest retailer of German wine in the UK and with wines from over 45 German vineyards there is something to suit every taste. The beautiful nineteenth century shelving also houses fantastic vintages from the shop's secondary specialist regions (France, Italy, Spain and California), all of which have been imported by The Winery direct from growers.

CONTACT

020 7286 6475
www.thewineryuk.com
info@thewineryuk.com
⊖ / ⇌ Warwick Avenue

OVERVIEW

First opened
1996
Owner
David Motion

WINE

No. available
650
Specialty
German wine

PRICING

Per bottle	£8 - £500
Av. bottle sold	£14

WINE MERCHANT DIRECTORY

WINE BROKERAGE, WHOLESALE AND PRIVATE CLIENT SALES				
VENUE	HEAD OFFICE	WEBSITE	TELEPHONE	EMAIL
Bibendum Wine	113 Regents Park Road, NW1 8UR	www.bibendum-wine.co.uk	0845 263 6924	N/A
Bordeaux Index	10 Hatton Garden, EC1N 8AH	www.bordeauxindex.com	020 7269 0703	sales@bordeauxindex.com
Farr Vintners	220 Queensntown Road, SW8 4LP	www.farrvintners.com	020 7821 2000	sales@farrvintners.com
Fine + Rare Wines	Woolyard, 54 Bermondsey Street, SE1 3UD	www.frw.co.uk	020 7089 7400	wine@frw.co.uk
Goedhuis & Co	Unit 6, Rudolf Place, SW8 1RP	www.goedhuis.com	020 7793 7900	sales@goedhuis.com
Imperial Wines of London	1 Poultry, EC2R 8JR	www.imperialwinesoflondon.com	0800 678 3117	enquiries@imperialwinesoflondon.com
Justerini & Brooks	61 St James's Street, SW1A 1LZ	www.justerinis.com	020 7484 6400	justorders@justerinis.com
Magnum Fine Wines	5 Conduit Street, W1S 2XD	www.magnum.co.uk	020 7629 5607	wine@magnum.co.uk
Wilkinson Vintners	38 Chagford Street, NW1 6EB	www.wilkinsonvintners.com	020 7616 0404	wine@wilkinsonvintners.com

NATIONWIDE MERCHANTS		
VENUE	FLAGSHIP STORE	WEBSITE
Laithwaites	Arch 219-221 Stoney Street, SE1 9AA	www.laithwaites.co.uk
Majestic	21a-23 Loudoun Road, NW8 0ND	www.majestic.co.uk
Nicolas	98 Holland Park Avenue, W11 3RB	www.nicolas.co.uk
Oddbins	7 Borough High Street, SE1 9SU	www.oddbins.com
Wine Rack	8-9 Bedford Corner, The Avenue, W4 1LD	www.winerack.co.uk

Wine Bars

We consider a wine bar to be somewhere where you can sit down for a glass of good wine with no requirement to order a meal. The wine bars in this section are recommended for their outstanding wine list, interesting concept or speciality.

Wine Bars

28°- 50° Wine Workshop & Kitchen

140 Fetter Lane, EC4A 1BT

Photo: John Carey

OPEN

Mon-Fri.	11:00am - 11:00pm
Sat-Sun.	Closed

ORGANIC

The 28°- 50° Wine Workshop & Kitchen is charming and informal, particularly for the City, and they aim to cover all bases. The "normal" wine list includes 15 red and 15 white wines by the glass, carafe or bottle, with the option of a 75ml taster measure. If you are out to impress, ask for the "collector" list of fine wines sourced from private cellars. In the unlikely event that neither list tempts you, there is the option to bring your own bottle for a £15 corkage fee (you need to arrange this with the bar in advance). In case you were wondering, the venue's name refers to the latitude at which most wines in the world are grown.

CONTACT

020 7242 8877
www.2850.co.uk
fetter@2850.co.uk
⊖ / ⇌ City Thameslink

Other London locations
Marylebone

OVERVIEW

First opened
2010
Owner
Xavier Rousset and Agnar Sverrisson

WINE

No. available
160
No. by the glass
43

PRICING

Per bottle	£19.50 - £495
Av. bottle sold	£28
Av. glass	£8 (125ml)

40 Maltby Street

40 Maltby Street, SE1 3PA

Operating from a London Bridge railway arch, Gergovie Wines is a merchant selling natural, organic wine from a handful of small European producers. For three evenings a week and on Saturday the warehouse opens as a bar, "40 Maltby Street", where you can try the wine and grab a bite to eat. The bar is rough and ready and not at all easy to find, so naturally it has a cult following. Most fans will tell you not to go so they can keep it to themselves. Don't be swayed, this place is a gem.

CONTACT

020 7237 9247
www.40maltbystreet.com
bar@maltbystreet.com
⊖ / ⇌ Bermondsey

OPEN

Mon-Tue & Sun.	Closed
Wed-Fri.	5:30pm - 10:00pm
Sat.	10:00am - 5:00pm

OVERVIEW

First opened
2011
Owner
Raef Hodgson and Harry Lester

WINE

No. available
20
No. by the glass
8
Specialty
Natural wine

PRICING

Per bottle	£21 - £58
Av. bottle sold	£25
Av. glass	£5.50 (125ml)

Bar Pepito

3 Varnishers Yard, N1 9FD

Bar Pepito is a wonderful Andalusian bodega specialising in Sherry, with over 15 types ranging from fino to sweet and everything in between. If you are new to Sherry or feeling indecisive then the "Sherry flights" are just the ticket. The small bar is friendly, fun and dedicated to its heritage. Try some of the Andalusian cheese for the complete experience.

CONTACT

020 7841 7331
www.camino.uk.com/pepito
barpepito@camino.uk.com
⊖ / ⇌ King's Cross / St Pancras

OPEN

Mon-Fri.	5:00pm - midnight
Sat.	6:00pm - midnight
Sun.	Closed

OVERVIEW

First opened
2010
Owner
Richard Bigg

WINE

No. available
33
No. by the glass
33
Specialty
Sherry

PRICING

Per bottle	£16 - £32
Av. bottle sold	£21
Av. glass	£4.50 (175ml)

Bedales

5 Bedale Street, SE1 9AL

A love of wine in its pure form has led Bedales to specialise in organic, biodynamic and natural wines. Bedales is particularly proud of the wines from its "Italian dreamers"; growers from across Italy, each of whom is representative of his respective region. Take a seat at one of the wine barrel tables lining the outside of the bar to watch Borough Market in action.

CONTACT

020 7403 8853
www.bedaleswines.com
tastings@bedaleswines.com
⊖ / ⇌ London Bridge

Other London locations
Spitalfields Market /
Leadenhall Market

OPEN

Mon-Tue.	10:00am - 10:00pm
Wed.	10:00am - 10:30pm
Thu-Fri.	10:00am - 11:00pm
Sat.	9:00am - 10:00pm
Sun.	10:00am - 7:00pm

OVERVIEW

First opened
2001
Owner
Bedales Enterprises Limited

WINE

No. available
150
No. by the glass
15
Specialty
French, Italian and organic wine

PRICING

Per bottle	£11 - £800
Av. bottle sold	£20
Av. glass	£6.50 (175ml)

Dalla Terra

25 Slingsby Place, WC2E 9AB

Tucked away in St Martin's Courtyard, this stylish Italian wine bar and shop provides a welcome escape from the hustle and bustle of Covent Garden. Choose any bottle off the shelf and settle into an Eames chair by the fire to complete the enoteca experience. With 30 cheeses on the menu, it is a superb opportunity to find your favourite Italian matches.

OPEN

Mon-Thu.	9:30am - 11:30pm
Fri-Sat.	9:30am - midnight
Sun.	9:30am - 10:30pm

OVERVIEW

First opened
March 2012
Owner
Giuseppe Gullo

WINE

No. available
300
No. by the glass
30
Specialty
Italian wine

PRICING

Per bottle	£15 - £250
Av. bottle sold	£30
Av. glass	£9 (125ml)

CONTACT

020 7240 8811
www.dallaterra.co.uk
info@dallaterra.co.uk
⊖ / ⇌ Covent Garden

Gordon's Wine Bar

47 Villiers Street, WC2N 6NE

Thought to be the oldest wine bar in London, Gordon's is also one of the most popular. Make your way down the creaky stairs from Villiers Street into the candle-lit cellar, snap up a table and join the regulars sipping Port, Sherry or Madeira from barrels behind the bar. Gordon's is always buzzing with post-work drinkers and the secluded alcoves are the perfect spot for a romantic, late night rendezvous.

OPEN

Mon-Sat.   11:00am - 11:00pm
Sun.   12:00pm - 10:00pm

OVERVIEW

First opened
1890
Owner
The Gordon Family

CONTACT

020 7930 1408
www.gordonswinebar.com
gerard@gordonswinebar.com
⊖ / ⇌ Embankment

WINE

No. available
125
No. by the glass
70
Specialty
Port and Madeira wine

PRICING

Per bottle	£16 - £120
Av. bottle sold	£19
Av. glass	£5 (125ml)

Kensington Wine Rooms

127-129 Kensington Church Street, W8 7LP

Image supplied by Kensington Wine Rooms

OPEN

Mon-Sun. 12:00pm - midnight

The sense of fun at this smart Notting Hill bar is complemented by the quirky artwork adorning the walls. Wines are available to order by the glass or bottle but we recommend you take the more adventurous route of topping up a wine "oyster" card from behind the bar. Try as many wines as you can from the 40 available in the enomatic tasting machines.

CONTACT

020 7727 8142
www.greatwinesbytheglass.com
enquiries@thekensingtonwinerooms.com
⊖ / ⇌ Notting Hill Gate

Other London locations
Fulham

OVERVIEW

First opened
2009
Owner
Thor Gudmundsson and Richard Okroj

....

WINE

No. available
200
No. by the glass
50
Specialty
Northern Rhône Syrah

PRICING

Per bottle	£19 - £215
Av. bottle sold	£40
Av. glass	£10 (175ml)

....

Le Beaujolais

25 Litchfield Street, WC2H 9NJ

OPEN

Mon-Fri.	12:00pm - 11:00pm
Sat.	5:00pm - 11:00pm
Sun.	Closed

Le Beaujolais is a charming combination of an old English pub and a French bistro in eclectic central Soho. Beer mugs and public school ties hang from the ceiling but the wine list is classically French, as is the small menu which includes croque monsieur, rillettes and boeuf bourguignon. Customers are treated like old friends and there are regulars who have been coming here since it opened 30 odd years ago.

CONTACT

020 7836 2955

⊖ / ⇌ Leicester Square

OVERVIEW

First opened
1981
Owner
Michel Grondin and Jean-Yves Darcel

WINE

No. available
60
No. by the glass
7
Specialty
Beaujolais

PRICING

Per bottle	£19 - £48
Av. bottle sold	£25
Av. glass	£5.50 (175ml)

Negozio Classica

154 Regents Park Road, NW1 8XN

Negozio Classica is a wine shop, bar and restaurant that offers a rustic Tuscan experience in a contemporary London setting. It is owned by a Montepulciano winery so the quality of the wine is high and many of the wines are exclusive to the store. You can choose any of the shop's bottles to drink on-site for a small corkage fee and plenty of the wines are also available by the glass at the bar.

OPEN

Mon-Thu.	3:30pm - 11:00pm
Fri.	11:00am - 11:30pm
Sat.	10:00am - 11:30pm
Sun.	11:00am - 11:00pm

OVERVIEW

First opened
2011
Owner
Virginie Saverys, Maximilien de Zarobe
and Marco Brustio

....

WINE

No. available
120
No. by the glass
25
Specialty
Italian wine

PRICING

Per bottle	£16.50 - £228
Av. bottle sold	£23
Av. glass	£7.50 (175ml)

....

CONTACT

020 7483 4492
www.negozioclassica.co.uk
info@negozioclassica.co.uk
⊖ / ⇄ Chalk Farm

Other London locations
Notting Hill

Searcys Champagne Bar at St Pancras

Grand Terrace, St. Pancras International Station, N1C 4QL

OPEN

Mon-Sat. 7:00am - 11:00pm
Sun. 8:00am - 11:00pm

Nothing sets you up for a journey like Champagne and this bar at St. Pancras International has more Champagne by the glass than any other in Europe. If you have plenty of time before your train, there are also over 100 bottles to choose from. On a clear day, the bar is sunlit through the beautiful arched glass roof. In winter, there are heated leather seats and blankets to keep you toasty until the Champagne does the trick.

CONTACT

020 7870 9900
www.searcyschampagnebars.co.uk
stpg@searcys.co.uk
⊖ / ⇌ King's Cross / St. Pancras

Other London locations
One New Change / Paddington / Westfield Stratford / Westfield White City

OVERVIEW

First opened
2007
Owner
Richard Tear and Christian Rose

WINE

No. available
180
No. by the glass
45
Specialty
Champagne

PRICING

Per bottle £19 - £1,500
Av. bottle sold £70 (Champagne) / £31 (other wine)
Av. glass £9 (125ml)

Vinopolis

No. 1 Bank End, SE1 9BU

Image supplied by Vinopolis

Vinopolis is not actually a wine bar but an educational wine and spirits tasting complex. The main event is a self-guided tour through the winery, which includes enomatic sampling of wine and interactive tuition about wine making. Experts are on hand to answer questions and each tour includes an introductory session on how to taste wine. The ticket price includes drinks tokens, which are redeemable against sampling within the experience, and additional tokens can be purchased at the venue. After the tour, test out your newly acquired knowledge in one of the many bars and restaurants within the complex, including Wine Wharf (featured on page 110). All the wines you taste on the tour are available to buy at the Vinopolis Laithwaites store. With nearly 7,000 bottles on-site, Vinopolis offers a complete wine tasting experience.

OVERVIEW

First opened
1999
Owner
Wineworld London Plc

CONTACT

020 7940 8300
www.vinopolis.co.uk
sales@vinopolis.co.uk
⊖ / ⇌ London Bridge

Vinoteca

15 Seymour Place, W1H 5BD

OPEN

Mon-Sat.	12:00pm - 11:00pm
Sun.	12:00pm - 5:00pm

Vinoteca may be decorated in the Art Nouveau style and inspired by traditional Mediterranean wine bars, but this venue takes a thoroughly modern approach to wine. The wine list is well-balanced between Old World and New, the familiar and unusual. Every bottle can be taken away at a retail price and the food menu complements wine available by the glass. Ask about Prosecco on tap and premium "Bag-in-Box" wines, which are fantastic value and environmentally friendly too. This venue is sure to impress even the most critical connoisseur.

CONTACT

020 7724 7288
www.vinoteca.co.uk
marylebone@vinoteca.co.uk
⊖ / ⇌ Marble Arch

Other London locations
Farringdon / Soho

OVERVIEW

First opened
2010
Owner
Charlie Young, Brett Woonton and Elena Ares

WINE

No. available
300
No. by the glass
25
Specialty
Italian and French wine

PRICING

Per bottle	£16 - £176
Av. bottle sold	£24
Av. glass	£5 (125ml)

Wine Wharf

Stoney Street, SE1 9AD

OPEN

Mon-Wed.	4:00pm - 11:00pm
Thu-Sat.	12:00pm - 11:00pm
Sun.	Closed

Part of the Vinopolis complex and next to Borough Market, Wine Wharf is a popular spot for City folk and market shoppers alike. The bar is located in a redeveloped Victorian warehouse, designed as "industrial chic" with exposed brickwork, clean steel and wood flooring. The international wine list is extensive and each label is accompanied by tasting notes for additional guidance. Pop in for a casual drink or pre-book a sommelier to tutor a private "wine experience".

CONTACT

020 7940 8335
www.winewharf.co.uk
vinumreservation2@vinopolis.co.uk
⊖ / ⇌ London Bridge

OVERVIEW

First opened
2000
Owner
Vinum Restaurant Company Ltd

....

WINE

No. available
160
No. by the glass
70
Specialty

PRICING

Per bottle	£19 - £900
Av. bottle sold	£25
Av. glass	£5 (125ml)

....

Food &
Wine Halls

London is home to some of the most iconic shopping centres in the world. Whether you are visiting for exclusive brands or specialist produce, everything is under one roof for your convenience.

Fortnum & Mason

181 Piccadilly, W1A 1ER

Fortnum & Mason is one of London's iconic stores and established its name 300 years ago, creating food hampers for the Georgian gentry. The beautiful food hall sells quintessential English delicacies including Fortnum's famous potted Stilton. The cheese counter offers the best of British and a few well-known cheeses from the Continent. The wine department is comprehensive in geographical scope, with a particularly impressive selection of Champagne and own label wines sourced from top growers. Take any of their bottles into the adjoining 1707 wine bar for a £10 corkage fee or experiment with one of the carefully crafted wine flights.

WINE

No. available
160
Specialty
Old World wine

PRICING
Per bottle   £9.50 - £1,400
Av. bottle sold   £16

OPEN

Mon-Sat.   10:00am - 9:00pm
Sun.   11:30am - 7:00pm

OVERVIEW

First opened
1707
Owner
The Weston Family

CONTACT

0845 300 1707
www.fortnumandmason.com
⊖ / ⇌ Green Park

CHEESE

No. available
140
Countries of origin
Britain, France, Ireland, Italy, Switzerland

PRICING per 100g

Brie de Meaux	£2.80
Mature Cheddar	£3.00
Parmigiano-Reggiano	£4.00
Stilton	£2.20

Greensmiths

27 Lower Marsh, SE1 7RG

Owner Chris Smith has created a dream
supermarket - high quality, fresh
produce displayed with care and
attention in a smartly designed store.
Meat comes from the Ginger Pig and
bread from Clapham's Old Post Office
Bakery. Head downstairs to find 100
affordable artisan wines supplied by
The Waterloo Wine Co. There is also a
comprehensive selection of 35 cheeses,
most of which come from Neal's Yard
Dairy. Located just next to Waterloo
Station, this is a fantastic grocery venue
for South Londoners.

WINE

No. available
100
Specialty
New Zealand wine

PRICING
Per bottle   £6 - £30
Av. bottle sold   £10

OPEN

Mon-Fri.	8:00am - 8:00pm
Sat.	8:00am - 6:00pm
Sun.	Closed

OVERVIEW

First opened
2008
Owner
Chris Smith

CONTACT

020 7921 2970
www.greensmithsfood.co.uk
enquiries@greensmithsfood.co.uk
⊖ / ⇄ Waterloo

CHEESE

No. available
30 - 40
Countries of origin
Britain, France, Italy, Netherlands,
Spain, Switzerland

PRICING per 100g
Brie de Meaux	£1.88
Parmigiano-Reggiano	£3.10
Stilton	£2.15

Harrods

87-135 Brompton Road, SW1X 7XL

[TOP 5]
IN CATEGORY

OPEN

Mon-Sat.	10:00am - 8:00pm
Sun.	12:00pm - 6:00pm

(opening times change seasonally)

Harrods recently revamped its wine department to offer "the complete wine experience". Eclectic wines sit alongside a sophisticated classic selection, there is a luxury tasting room, a bar serving fantastic wine flights and a new interactive "aroma zone". The cheese counter in Harrods' exquisite food hall is arranged by type of cheese, rather than country, making it easy to find what you are after. The focus is on traditional cheeses and pride of place is given to a whole drum of Gorgonzola, specially selected for Harrods and matured for 120 days.

WINE

No. available
3,200
No. to sample
16

PRICING

Per sample	£1 - £5
Per bottle	£7 - £9,000

OVERVIEW

First opened
1849
Owner
The Qatari Royal Family

CONTACT

020 7730 1234
www.harrods.com
 / ⇌ Knightsbridge

CHEESE

No. available
135
Countries of origin
Britain, France, Germany, Ireland, Italy, Netherlands, Spain, Switzerland

PRICING per 100g

Brie de Meaux	£2.65
Mature Cheddar	£1.25 - £3.25
Parmigiano-Reggiano	£3.75
Stilton	£2.00 - £2.49

Harvey Nichols

109-125 Knightsbridge, SW1X 7RJ

OPEN

Mon-Sat.	10:00am - 8:00pm
Sun.	12:00pm - 8:00pm

OVERVIEW

First opened
1831
Owner
Dickson Poon

CONTACT

020 7235 5000
www.harveynichols.com
personalshopping-knightsbridge@
harveynichols.com
⊖ / ⤫ Knightsbridge

The towering shelves in Harvey Nichols' wine department house an excellent range of well-known names, particularly from the Old World. You will also find vintages from small-scale producers, an artistically designed house range and sophisticated fine wine selection. The cheese counter is small, with a few gems nestled amongst the Brie and Cheddar – look out for Caciotta Etrusca (an unusual Pecorino) and Napoléon (a nutty ewe's milk cheese from the Pyrenees).

CHEESE

No. available
25
Countries of origin
Britain, France, Italy, Spain

WINE

No. available
800

PRICING

Per bottle	£7.50 - £7,500
Av. bottle sold	£29

PRICING per 100g

Brie de Meaux	£2.35
Mature Cheddar	£2.40
Parmigiano-Reggiano	£3.45
Stilton	£2.10

John Lewis foodhall from Waitrose

300 Oxford Street, W1A 1EX

Food & Wine Halls

OPEN

Mon-Wed & Fri-Sat.	9:30am - 8:00pm
Thu.	9.30am - 9.00pm
Sun.	12.00pm - 6.00pm

With three Masters of Wine on its buying team, Waitrose takes wine seriously. Amongst bottles for everyday drinking you will find the largest range of English wines in London and an "Inner Cellar" of exceptional vintages. The Cheese Room's extensive range offers a mix of pre-cut and counter service. The focus is artisan British cheese but you will also find some very interesting Continental cheeses, many of which are labelled by strength of flavour with information about the cheese.

OVERVIEW

First opened
2007
Owner
The John Lewis staff

CONTACT

020 7629 7711
www.johnlewis.com
⊖ / ⇌ Oxford Circus / Bond Street

Other London locations
45 London Waitrose stores

WINE

No. available
550
Specialty
English wine

PRICING

Per bottle	£4 - £750
Av. bottle sold	£10

CHEESE

No. available
250
Countries of origin
Britain, France, Germany, Ireland, Italy, Netherlands, Spain, Switzerland

PRICING per 100g

Brie de Meaux	£1.76
Mature Cheddar	£2.70
Parmigiano-Reggiano	£2.45
Stilton	£1.75

Partridges

2-5 Duke of York Square, SW3 4LY

Partridges is a food haven for its Chelsea residents and a one-stop-shop for a high end dinner party. The cheese cabinet is packed with varieties from across Europe but specialises in French cheese: take the opportunity to ask staff for an alternative to your usual Brie de Meaux. With ingredients and cheese sorted, head to the wine department for a bottle to match your meal. Look past the classics to find some new and unique names that will entice you away from the old favourites.

....

WINE

No. available
800
Specialty
Rioja

PRICING
Per bottle	£7 - £69
Av. bottle sold	£9

....

OPEN
Mon-Sun.   8:00am - 10:00pm

OVERVIEW
First opened
1972
Owner
John Shepherd

CONTACT
020 7730 0651
www.partridges.co.uk
enquiries@partridges.co.uk
⊖ / ⇌ Sloane Square

Other London locations
Gloucester Road

....

CHEESE
No. available
130
Countries of origin
Britain, France, Ireland, Italy, Netherlands, Scandinavia, Spain, Switzerland

PRICING per 100g
Brie de Meaux	£2.50
Mature Cheddar	£1.90 - £2.55
Parmigiano-Reggiano	£2.50
Stilton	£2.50

....

Selfridges

[TOP 5]
IN CATEGORY

400 Oxford Street, W1A 1AB

OPEN

Mon-Fri.	9:30am - 9:00pm
Sat.	9:30am - 10:00pm
Sun.	10:00am - 9:00pm

(opening times change seasonally)

The Selfridges wine department is part of the famous Wonder Room, aptly named for its display of conspicuous luxury. The offering from France, Spain, Australia and the Americas is particularly strong and there is ample choice of big named wines as well as those from smaller producers.
Taste some of the wines at the Wonder Bar, then return to the department and buy your favourite. The cheese counter is brimming with a delectable seasonal selection that covers most of Europe. Traditional cheeses are interspersed with newer ones and blackboards on the wall provide inspiration to help you choose.

OVERVIEW

First opened
1909
Owner
Galen Weston

CONTACT

0800 123 400
www.selfridges.com
customerservices@selfridges.com
⊖ / ⇌ Bond Street

CHEESE

No. available
115
Countries of origin
Britain, France, Ireland, Italy, Netherlands, Scandinavia, Spain, Switzerland

WINE

No. available
1,000
No. to sample
52
Specialty
Small-producer wine

PRICING

Per sample	£1 - £45
Per bottle	£7 - £3,000
Av. bottle sold	£18

PRICING per 100g

Brie de Meaux	£2.30
Mature Cheddar	£2.65
Parmigiano-Reggiano	£3.50
Stilton	£2.30

Whole Foods Market

63-97 Kensington High Street, W8 5SE

OPEN

Mon-Sat.   8:00am - 10:00pm
Sun.   12:00pm - 8:00pm

Whole Foods has a dedicated cheese room with a wide selection of British and Continental artisan cheeses. Most of the cheeses are pre-cut so there is no need for counter service, but friendly cheesemongers are on hand if you require help. There are almost 1,000 bottles of wine on display, clearly arranged and labelled. Trained sommeliers are more than happy to provide advice or you can sample some of the 24 wines available at "The Wine Hub" tasting area.

OVERVIEW

First opened
2007
Owner
John Mackey

CONTACT

020 7368 4500
www.wholefoodsmarket.com
⊖ / ⇌ High Street Kensington

Other London locations
Camden / Clapham / Piccadilly / Stoke Newington

WINE

No. available
1,000
No. to sample
24
Specialty
Organic and natural wine

PRICING

Per sample	£0.50 - £9
Per bottle	£6 - £300
Av. bottle sold	£12

CHEESE

No. available
250
Countries of origin
Britain, France, Germany, Ireland, Italy, Netherlands, Spain, Switzerland

PRICING per 100g

Brie de Meaux	£1.69
Mature Cheddar	£1.39
Parmigiano-Reggiano	£3.79
Stilton	£2.69

Food & Wine Halls

Restaurants

London is famed for its restaurant wine lists, and has no shortage of impressive cheese boards either. Each of our chosen restaurants has an exceptional cheese *and* wine offering, whether it forms part of a meal or can be enjoyed as a standalone service.

1901

Andaz Liverpool Street, 40 Liverpool Street, EC2M 7QN

The bustle of the City instantly melts away as you enter this stunning Neoclassical dining room. A cabinet at the back of the room showcases British cheeses and a selection of the restaurant's 400 vintages. Dedicated cheese and wine fans can opt for a bespoke group tasting experience at a special tasting table. Four different types of cheese board are prepared and you can either match the wines yourself or ask the sommelier to choose them for you. Canapés and tapas dishes created specifically to accompany the tasting are an optional extra.

WINE

No. available
400
No. by the glass
50
No. bottles under £35
60

PRICING
Per bottle	£21 - £1,600
Av. bottle sold	£45
Av. glass	£8.50 (175ml)

OPEN
Lunch
Mon-Fri.	12:00pm - 2:30pm
Sat-Sun.	Closed

Dinner
Mon-Sat.	6:30pm - 10:00pm
Sun.	Closed

OVERVIEW
First opened
1901
Owner
Hyatt International
Head Chef
Michael Kreiling
Three courses
£45

CONTACT
020 7618 7000
www.andazdining.com/1901
london.restres@andaz.com
⊖ / ⇌ Liverpool Street

CHEESE
No. available
15 - 20
Countries of origin
Britain

PRICING
Whole cheese board	£11

The Bingham

61-63 Petersham Road, TW10 6UT

Perched on the leafy banks of the Thames in Richmond, The Bingham's beautiful location is reason enough to visit. The wine list is varied, whilst displaying the sommelier's penchant for Pinot Noir and Chardonnay, and includes a few affordable bottles. The cheese counter displays around 15 traditional cheeses from which you can choose up to five, all sourced from The Teddington Cheese. Combine your cheese and wine with a critically-acclaimed meal in the restaurant or enjoy on their own in the boutique bar overlooking the garden and river.

....

WINE

No. available
320
No. by the glass
29
No. bottles under £35
40
Speciality
Pinot Noir and Chardonnay

PRICING
Per bottle	£19 - £850
Av. bottle sold	£40
Av. glass	£9 (175ml)

....

OPEN

Lunch
Mon-Sat.	12:00pm - 2:30pm
Sun.	12:30pm - 4:00pm

Dinner
Mon-Wed.	7:00pm - 10:00pm
Thu.	6:30pm - 10:00pm
Fri-Sat.	6:30pm - 10:30pm
Sun.	Closed

OVERVIEW

First opened
2007
Owner
Ruth and Samantha Trinder
Head Chef
Shay Cooper
Three courses
£45

CONTACT

020 8940 0902
www.thebingham.co.uk
info@thebingham.co.uk
⊖ / ⇌ Richmond

....

CHEESE

No. available
15
Countries of origin
Britain, France, Switzerland

PRICING
Whole cheese board
Included if ordered as a pudding /
£8 as an additional course /
£11 without dinner

....

Brawn

49 Columbia Road, E2 7RG

Brawn has a chilled out café vibe with white-washed walls, retro furniture and a turntable behind the bar. The wine list offers natural biodynamic wines from France and Italy, which possess individuality and typify regional terroir. The four unusual cheeses on the menu are supplied by Androuet and change regularly. Staff receive training from Les Caves de Pyrene and Androuet, and will be happy to talk you through the wine and cheese selection.

WINE

No. available
150
No. by the glass
21
No. bottles under £35
70
Speciality
Natural wine

PRICING
Per bottle	£17 - £79.50
Av. bottle sold	£27
Av. glass	£6 (175ml)

OPEN
Lunch
Mon.	Closed
Tue-Sat.	12:00pm - 3:00pm
Sun.	12:00pm - 4:00pm

Dinner
Mon-Sat.	6:00pm - 11:00pm
Sun.	Closed

OVERVIEW
First opened
2010
Owner
Ed Woodson, Oliver Barker and Les Caves de Pyrene
Head Chef
Ed Woodson
Three courses
£23

CONTACT
020 7729 5692
www.brawn.co
enquiries@brawn.co
⊖ / ⇌ Bethnal Green
Sister Restaurants
Soif / Terroirs

CHEESE
No. available
4
Countries of origin
Britain, France

PRICING
Individual cheeses	£3.50
Whole cheese board	£10

Chez Bruce

2 Bellevue Road, SW17 7EG

Chez Bruce is a rare find in London – a restaurant that offers Michelin-starred food at reasonable prices in an informal setting. It is also one of London's top wine destinations, admired by wine novices and experts alike. The wine list features wine from 18 countries and includes a good selection of affordable bottles and familiar styles alongside lesser-known and fine vintages. One look at the famous cheese board, supplied by La Fromagerie and Neal's Yard Dairy, and you will forget all about pudding. Choose as many cheeses as you like and ask the sommelier for wine matching suggestions.

WINE

No. available
700
No. by the glass
40
No. bottles under £35
60

PRICING
Per bottle	£21 - £1,350
Av. glass	£7 (125ml)

OPEN

Lunch
Mon-Fri.	12:00pm - 2:30pm
Sat-Sun.	12:00pm - 3:00pm

Dinner
Mon-Thu.	6:30pm - 10:00pm
Fri-Sat.	6:30pm - 10:30pm
Sun.	7:00pm - 9:30pm

OVERVIEW

First opened
1995
Owner
Bruce Poole and Nigel Platts-Martin
Head Chef
Matt Christmas
Three courses
Lunch £27.50 / Dinner £45

CONTACT

020 8672 0114
www.chezbruce.co.uk
enquiries@chezbruce.co.uk
⊖ / ⇌ Wandsworth Common
Sister Restaurants
The Glasshouse / La Trompette

CHEESE

No. available
20 - 25
Countries of origin
Britain, France, Germany, Ireland, Italy, Spain, Switzerland

PRICING
Whole cheese board
£5 supplement /
£10 - £12.50 as an additional course

High Timber

8 High Timber Street, EC4V 3PA

High Timber's South African owners have infused the restaurant with local flavour, from the popular homemade biltong to the predominantly Western Cape wine. The cellars house an astonishing 40,000 bottles and you can choose your own bottle from the whole collection. The cheeses are mainly British and French and live in a small display room shared with the biltong. The contemporary dining room has incredible views across the Thames of the Globe and Tate Modern, providing the perfect backdrop to your visit.

WINE

No. available
2,000
No. by the glass
2,000
No. bottles under £35
600
Specialty
South African wine

PRICING
Per bottle	£19.50 - £5,000
Av. bottle sold	£45
Av. glass	£10 (175ml)

OPEN

Lunch
Mon-Fri.	12:00pm - 3:00pm
Sat-Sun.	Closed

Dinner
Mon-Fri.	6:30pm - 10:30pm
Sat-Sun.	Closed

OVERVIEW

First opened
2009
Owner
Gary & Kathy Jordan, Neleen Strauss
Head Chef
Justin Saunders
Three courses
£38

CONTACT

020 7248 1777
www.hightimber.com
info@hightimber.com
⊖ / ⇌ Mansion House

CHEESE

No. available
10 - 15
Countries of origin
Britain, France, Italy, Spain

PRICING
Individual cheeses   Priced by weight
Whole cheese board   From £7.50

L'Art du Fromage

1A Langton Street, SW10 0JL

Image supplied by L'Art du Fromage

Any turophile is bound to be excited on discovering London's only restaurant dedicated to cheese. The L'Art du Fromage menu includes two different types of fondue, a raclette and a tartiflette Savoyarde. For a real challenge, the fondue and raclette are "all you can eat". If you prefer a cheese board, owner Julien Ledogar will be on hand to help you choose from the extensive selection and advise on a complementary wine from an exclusively French list, which has been designed with cheese pairing in mind.

WINE

No. available
36
No. by the glass
14
No. bottles under £35
22
Specialty
French wine

PRICING
Per bottle	£18 - £87
Av. bottle sold	£27
Av. glass	£5.50 (175ml)

OPEN
Lunch
Mon & Sun.	Closed
Tue-Sat.	12:00pm - 3:30pm

Dinner
Mon-Sat.	6:30pm - 11:30pm
Sun.	Closed

OVERVIEW
First opened
2010
Owner
Julien Ledogar
Three courses
£30

CONTACT
020 7352 2759
www.artdufromage.co.uk
info@artdufromage.co.uk
⊖ / ⇌ Fulham Broadway / Sloane Square

CHEESE
No. available
45
Countries of origin
France, Switzerland

PRICING
Whole cheese board   £25.20

Le Gavroche

43 Upper Brook Street, W1K 7QR

OPEN

Lunch

Mon-Fri.	12:00pm - 2:00pm
Sat-Sun.	Closed

Dinner

Mon-Sat.	6:30pm - 11:00pm
Sun.	Closed

Holding two Michelin stars, Le Gavroche is one of London's great fine dining institutions. The renowned wine list is predominantly French, with mature vintages from some of the world's most prestigious wine makers. The cheese at Le Gavroche is equally impressive. Begin your meal with the restaurant's sensational signature dish: a twice-baked Gruyère and Cheddar soufflé on double cream. Conclude proceedings with a selection of exquisite cheeses supplied by Parisian affineur, Jacques Vernier.

OVERVIEW

First opened
1967
Owner
Michel Roux Jr.
Head Chef
Rachel Humphrey
Three courses
£92

CONTACT

020 7408 0881
www.le-gavroche.co.uk
bookings@le-gavroche.com
⊖ / ⇌ Marble Arch

WINE

No. available
800
No. by the glass
60
No. bottles under £35
25
Specialty
Bordeaux and Burgundy

PRICING

Per bottle	£29 - £19,450
Av. bottle sold	£50
Av. glass	£12 (175ml)

CHEESE

No. available
30 - 35
Countries of origin
Britain, France

PRICING

Whole cheese board
Included in set lunch and tasting menu /
£17.20 as an additional course

The Ledbury

127 Ledbury Road, W11 2AQ

The Ledbury holds two Michelin stars and consistently impresses with excellent food and service. The wine list is particularly strong for vintages from the Rhône valley, Burgundy and Bordeaux. There is also an extensive selection of sweet wines, with a focus on Riesling and a couple of very old Roussillon. The Ledbury's eclectic cheese selection, mainly supplied by La Fromagerie, will excite any turophile. With 30 vintages available by the glass, why not conclude your meal with some experimental cheese and wine pairings?

WINE

No. available
700
No. by the glass
28
No. bottles under £35
20
Specialty
Burgundy

PRICING
Per bottle	£24 - £2,750
Av. bottle sold	£70
Av. glass	£12 (175ml)

OPEN

Lunch
Mon.	Closed
Tue-Sat.	12:00pm - 2:00pm
Sun.	12:00pm - 2:30pm

Dinner
Mon-Sat.	6:30pm - 10:15pm
Sun.	7:00pm - 10:00pm

OVERVIEW
First opened
2005
Owner
Nigel Platts-Martin, Brett Graham and Philip Howard
Head Chef
Brett Graham
Three courses
£80

CONTACT
020 7792 9090
www.theledbury.com
info@theledbury.com
⊖ / ⇌ Westbourne Park
Sister Restaurants
The Square

CHEESE
No. available
10
Countries of origin
Britain, France, Germany, Italy, Switzerland

PRICING
Whole cheese board
£9 supplement /
£15 as an additional course

Marcus Wareing at The Berkeley

Wilton Place, SW1X 7RL

The sophistication of Marcus Wareing's superb, Michelin-starred food is mirrored in The Berkeley's smart and atmospheric dining room. The wine list is predominantly French, although you will find a good worldwide selection. Wines are chosen to complement the cuisine and are sourced from known makers and smaller vineyards. Beautiful cheeses from La Fromagerie are displayed in the centre of the restaurant to tempt you throughout the meal.

....

WINE

No. available
850
No. by the glass
26
No. bottles under £35
None
Specialty
French wine

PRICING
Per bottle	£35 - £21,500
Av. bottle sold	£70
Av. glass	£14 (175ml)

....

OPEN
Lunch

Mon-Fri.	12:00pm - 2:30pm
Sat-Sun.	Closed

Dinner

Mon-Sat.	6:00pm - 11:00pm
Sun.	Closed

OVERVIEW

First opened
2008
Owner
Marcus Wareing Restaurants
Head Chef
Marcus Wareing / Mark Froydenlund
Three courses
£80

CONTACT
020 7235 1200
www.marcus-wareing.com
marcuswareing@the-berkeley.co.uk
⊖ / ⇌ Knightsbridge /
Hyde Park Corner

....

CHEESE

No. available
15
Countries of origin
Britain, France, Germany, Italy, Spain

PRICING
Whole cheese board	£12

....

Medlar

438 King's Road, SW10 0LJ

[TOP 5] IN CATEGORY

Medlar is admired by critics and diners alike, inspired by the exceptional cooking and reasonable prices. Medlar aims to become one of London's top wine destinations and presents a well-considered, balanced list with a slight French emphasis, and many wines available by the carafe as well as the glass. Select as many cheeses as you like from the trolley brought to your table and if you are keen to test your palate then ask for the 24-month aged Gruyère, supplied in restricted quantities by the master fromager Bernard Antony.

WINE

No. available
450
No. by the glass
20
No. bottles under £35
67
Specialty
Bordeaux and Burgundy

PRICING
Per bottle   £21 - £590
Av. bottle sold   £55
Av. glass   £8 (125ml)

OPEN
Lunch
Mon-Sun.   12:00pm - 3:00pm

Dinner
Mon-Sun.   6:30pm - 10:30pm

OVERVIEW
First opened
2011
Owner
Joe Mercer Nairne and David O'Connor
Head Chef
Joe Mercer Nairne
Three courses
Lunch £25 / Dinner £39.50
(weekend prices vary)

CONTACT
020 7349 1900
www.medlarrestaurant.co.uk
info@medlarrestaurant.co.uk
⊖ / ⇌ Fulham Broadway /
Sloane Square

CHEESE
No. available
20 - 30
Countries of origin
Britain, France, Ireland, Italy,
Portugal, Spain

PRICING
Whole cheese board
£4 supplement /
£10 as an additional course

The Square

6-10 Bruton Street, W1J 6PU

Owner Philip Howard is considered one of the finest chefs in London and The Square has held two Michelin stars since 1998. The 90-page wine list is well-constructed with a focus on fine Old World vintages, so you may wish to consult a helpful sommelier before investing in a bottle. The cheese trolley is laden with mouth-watering cheeses in perfect condition, supplied by Paxton & Whitfield. As well as hosting the old favourites, the trolley includes a few unusual suspects for the more adventurous cheese fan.

WINE

No. available
1,300
No. by the glass
30
No. bottles under £35
15
Specialty
French wine

PRICING

Per bottle	£20 - £7,000
Av. bottle sold	£150
Av. glass	£13 (175ml)

OPEN

Lunch
Mon-Sat. 12:00pm - 2:45pm
Sun. Closed

Dinner
Mon-Thu. 6:30pm - 10:00pm
Fri & Sat. 6:30pm - 10:30pm
Sun. 6:30pm - 9:30pm

OVERVIEW

First opened
1991
Owner
Philip Howard
Head Chef
Robert Weston
Three courses
£80

CONTACT

020 7495 7100
www.squarerestaurant.com
reception@squarerestaurant.com
⊖ / ⇌ Bond Street / Green Park
Sister restaurants
The Ledbury

CHEESE

No. available
30
Countries of origin
Britain, France

PRICING
Whole cheese board
£10 supplement /
£15 as an additional course

135

Vivat Bacchus Restaurant and Wine Cellar

47 Farringdon Street, EC4A 4LL

At this City-based restaurant, there are wine flights with matching cheeses, a monthly cheese selection with matching wines, three suggested regional cheese boards, weekly tasting events and wine dinners featuring a cheese course.
You can also choose your own cheese board from the international cheese room. Look beyond the wine list and hand-pick your bottle from the cellar of 1,000 bins, a third of which are South African. Many of the wines are aged on site, so there is a good selection of older vintages.

WINE

No. available
1,000
No. by the glass
30
No. bottles under £35
40
Specialty
South African wine

PRICING
Per bottle   £16.50 - £15,000
Av. bottle sold   £38
Av. glass   £7 (175ml)

OPEN

Mon-Fri.	12:00pm - 11:30pm
Sat-Sun.	Closed

OVERVIEW

First opened
2003
Owner
Gerrie Knoetze
Head Chef
Fred Demary
Three courses
£30

CONTACT

020 7353 2648
www.vivatbacchus.co.uk
info@vivatbacchus.co.uk
⊖ / ⇌ Farringdon
Sister restaurants
Vivat Bacchus at London Bridge

CHEESE

No. available
45
Countries of origin
Britain, France, Ireland, Italy, Spain, Switzerland

PRICING
Individual cheeses   Priced by weight
Whole cheese board   From £9.40

Tasting
Cheese & Wine

Cheese Categories

Cheeses are often grouped according to certain characteristics they possess or how they have been made. Using categories can be helpful to describe the type of cheese you want to buy or are serving to guests, but it can also be confusing because there is no standardised system of categorisation. Everyone in the trade uses slightly different groups so if you are not sure of the group then just describe the cheese as fully as possible.

To keep things simple, we have only listed six broad cheese categories but you may come across others or see cheeses placed in a different category altogether.

Fresh Cheese

Fresh cheeses are matured for no longer than a couple of days, if at all, and do not have any rind. As a result, they tend to be fragile, soft, moist and white. Examples include Mascarpone, Ricotta, Feta, Childwickbury and Innes Button.

Soft Cheese

Soft cheeses are young with a typical maturing process lasting from around seven days to four weeks. They are characterised by a thin, delicate rind which is usually wrinkled or bumpy. If the cheese has been rolled in ash, as with some goat's milk cheeses, then it may also be blue-grey in colour. The cheese inside is moist but can be oozy, chalky, fudgy, creamy or all of these depending on how it has been made.

Most of the cheeses in this group are goat's milk cheeses, for example Tymsboro, Mothais-sur-Feuille, Chabichou du Poitou, Sainte-Maure de Touraine and Monte Enebro. We have also included some non-goat's milk cheeses such as Brillat-Savarin, Saint-Félicien, St Jude and Robiola alta Langa.

Some older goat's milk cheeses have a strong "goaty" aroma whilst others are fresh and citrusy. Non-goat's milk cheeses in this group tend to be buttery and light, unless they are triple-cream cheeses, like Brillat-Savarin, in which case they are rich and creamy.

Semi-Soft Cheese

The cheeses in this category often (although not always) have a soft and velvety white mould rind, known as a "bloomy" rind. The paste can be chalky and firm when the cheese is young, becoming oozy when it is ripe. Generally, semi-soft cheeses are matured for between one to two months. When made with cow's milk, these cheeses often have mushroomy or vegetal flavours and the rind has a slightly astringent taste. A ewe's milk cheese like Wigmore is milky and unctuous. In this category we include cheeses such as Brie de Meaux, Fougerus, Camembert, Tunworth, Wigmore, Azeitão and Serra da Estrela.

Hard Cheese

This category includes a large range of cheeses from those with a supple texture such as Abondance and Emmental through firmer cheeses like Wensleydale and Gouda to the hardest cheeses like Grana Padano and Old Winchester.

This category can be sub-divided, so you may see cheese with a supple paste described as "semi-hard". Sometimes, cheeses are distinguished because the milk has been heated during the cheesemaking process or the curd has been "pressed".

Hard cheeses often have complex flavours that develop over a long maturing process from several months to a few years. Typical flavours are earthy, nutty and tangy, with traditional mature Cheddar being a classic example of this. Northern "territorial" cheeses like Cheshire and Lancashire have an earthy, salty taste, reflecting the terroir of the region, whilst the mountain cheeses such as Comté and Napoléon have a distinct nuttiness. Mature Gouda and its relatives like Olde Remeker and Coolea, have strong notes of butterscotch, caramel and even chocolate. Ewe's milk cheeses like Berkswell, Pecorino and Manchego have a complex lactic taste and the classic Italian cheeses, Parmigiano-Reggiano and Grana Padano, have sweet, rich and fruity flavours.

Blue Cheese

Blue cheeses are easy to identify by the blue-green veins, which run through the cheese. The rind is usually greyish or orangey brown and can be either wet or dusty. The paste is moist and varies in colour from almost white (Harbourne Blue) to cream (Perl Las) and pale yellow (Barkham Blue). Some blue cheeses are buttery and mild like Gorgonzola Dolce and Beenleigh Blue. Others are peppery and tangy, such as Colston Bassett Stilton, or complex and creamy like Stichelton. Roquefort is spicy and salty and the Spanish blue, Cabrales, is possibly the spiciest of all.

Washed Rind

During the maturing process, these cheeses are washed regularly in brine and often a wine or spirit made locally to the dairy. The rind develops a pinkish-orangey-brown colour and becomes sticky. Washed rind cheeses are known for their pungent aroma, which some people find off-putting. The paste inside, however, can be mild and creamy or rich and sweet. Examples of washed rind cheeses include Stinking Bishop, Oxford Isis, Ardrahan, Epoisses, Reblochon, Mahón and Taleggio.

From the Cheese Shop to Your Table

Buying Cheese

• If there is a large selection of cheeses available in the shop, take your time and ask the cheesemonger lots of questions - chances are they love talking about cheese.

• Is your cheese for a dinner party at the weekend, a sandwich lunch that day or a gift for next week? Tell your cheesemonger and they will suggest cheese to match the occasion as well as the right quantity and level of ripeness.

• Each artisan cheese tastes different because it has been handmade. Many factors influence the taste of artisan cheese including the weather, how far the milk has travelled to the cheesemaker, whether the cheese has been matured and how it has been stored. Even if you know the cheese well, it is worth having a taste in the shop to make sure the piece you are about to buy is exactly what you are after. If it is not to your satisfaction then explain why so you can be guided to a cheese you prefer.

• The cheese you buy may be wrapped without a label. If you are unsure of its name, ask your cheesemonger to write it down so you know what to look for next time.

Storage

• Cheese keeps best when it is whole and whole cheeses will continue to mature, although cold temperatures slow down the maturing process.

• Cut cheese does not continue to mature, so a slice of Brie will not ripen in your fridge although it may become softer.

• The ideal place to store cheese is somewhere cool and damp. A garage, shed or cellar may be suitable so long as the temperature is stable and relatively cool (but not too cold).

• If you store cheese in the fridge, place it on top of a damp cloth in an air-tight container. The container should be kept in the least cold part of the fridge, which is usually the salad drawer.

• Blue cheese should be kept in a separate container from your other cheese to prevent cross-contamination of the blue mould.

• Waxed paper is a good material for storing cheese at home and often provided by the cheese shop. If you do not have waxed paper, you can wrap the cheese in cling-film but leave the rind uncovered so it can breathe. It is better to wrap moist blue cheese in foil rather than cling-film. Replace the waxed paper, cling-film or foil with a new piece each time you take out your cheese.

• Soft cheeses should keep for a few days whilst hard cheeses can last for up to two weeks, although this will depend on the conditions in which the cheese is kept. If your hard cheese develops mould then you can cut it off and keep the cheese. New mould on the outside of a softer cheese can also be fine but throw the cheese away if you are in any doubt as to whether it is still good to eat.

Serving Cheese

• Allow your cheese to come to room temperature before you eat it. If you store cheese in the fridge, this may take up to two hours. Remove your cheese from its wrapping and place it on a board, covered with a damp cloth, while it warms up.

• Most cheese lovers, quite understandably, do not have the full array of cheese knives. Whilst these are fun, they are not really necessary - any sharp knife will do. If you serve a selection of cheeses it is best to cut each one with a different knife. If this is not possible then wash the knife in a bowl of warm water in between cutting the cheeses. This prevents the flavours of the cheese mixing as you work round the cheese board. At the very least, a clean knife should be used for any blue cheese to make sure there is no cross-contamination of the blue mould, which could ruin the other cheeses if they are put back in storage for another occasion.

• If you are eating a selection of cheeses then start with the mildest first. This is usually a goat's milk cheese if one is included on the board. Finish with the strongest cheese. If you have a blue cheese on your board then this should be eaten last. Our suggested cheese boards can be found on page 143.

• Can you eat the rind? Well, it depends. If the rind is covered with wax or cheese mites, for example Gouda and Mimolette, then we would not recommend it. However, the springy bloomy rind of a Brie or Camembert adds flavour and complexity to the cheese and can be delicious if it is in a good condition. Similarly, the pungent and salty washed rind of a cheese like Epoisses or Taleggio will be a delight for fans of strong cheese. If in doubt, just have a nibble of the rind and see if you like it...

• Did you know that Parmigiano rind can be added to soup, stock or sauce to add depth of flavour? Just remember to retrieve the melted rind before you serve.

Cheese Boards

A cheese board is the perfect way to taste several different cheeses in one sitting.

A selection of four to six cheeses provides a good range without being over-complicated. The traditional cheese board comprises a goat's milk cheese, soft or semi-soft cheese, hard cheese and a blue. You could also create a board by geographical region, type of milk or strength of flavour. Use the opportunity to experiment with taste and texture and to try some new cheeses.

Here are some of our favourite regional cheese boards, arranged with the mildest cheese first and finishing with the blue. We suggest the best way to serve a cheese board on page 142.

BRITISH TRADITIONAL

1. **Gorwydd Caerphilly**
   (cow's milk, hard)
2. **Appleby's Red Cheshire**
   (cow's milk, hard)
3. **Mrs Kirkham's Lancashire**
   (cow's milk, hard)
4. **Montgomery's Cheddar**
   (cow's milk, hard)
5. **Colston Bassett Stilton**
   (cow's milk, blue)

BRITISH MODERN

1. **Dorstone**
   (goat's milk, soft)
2. **Berkswell**
   (ewe's milk, hard)
3. **Tunworth**
   (cow's milk, semi-soft)
4. **Lincolnshire Poacher**
   (cow's milk, hard)
5. **Cardo**
   (goat's milk, washed rind)
6. **Stichelton**
   (cow's milk, blue)

FRENCH STRONG

1. **Pouligny-St-Pierre**
   (goat's milk, soft)
2. **Saint-Marcellin**
   (cow's milk, soft)
3. **24 month Comté**
   (cow's milk, hard)
4. **Epoisses**
   (cow's milk, washed rind)
5. **Roquefort**
   (ewe's milk, blue)

FRENCH MILD

1. **Selles-sur-Cher**
   (goat's milk, soft)
2. **Ossau Iraty**
   (ewe's milk, hard)
3. **Beaufort d'Alpage**
   (cow's milk, hard)
4. **Fougerus**
   (cow's milk, semi-soft)
5. **Saint-Nectaire**
   (cow's milk, hard)
6. **Fourme d'Ambert**
   (cow's milk, blue)

SPANISH & PORTUGUESE

1. **Monte Enebro**
   (goat's milk, soft)
2. **Payoyo**
   (goat and ewe's milk, hard)
3. **Serra da Estrela**
   (ewe's milk, semi-soft)
4. **Manchego Curado**
   (ewe's milk, hard)
5. **Picos de Europa**
   (cow's milk plus goat
   and ewe's milk, blue)

ITALIAN

1. **Caprino Caprissima**
   (goat's milk, fresh)
2. **Robiola alta Langa**
   (triple milk, soft)
3. **Piave Vecchio**
   (cow's milk, hard)
4. **Taleggio**
   (cow's milk, washed rind)
5. **Gorgonzola Piccante**
   (cow's milk, blue)

How to Taste Wine

Appearance

• Always hold a wine glass by its stem or base. This allows you to see the wine properly and prevents the wine warming in your hand.

• The best way to check the wine's clarity is to hold the glass at an angle against a white background.

• Generally, the wine should be clear and bright to indicate that it is in good condition. However, lack of clarity does not always mean the wine is tainted. Natural wines (which are not filtered) and aged wines (where sediment has formed during the ageing process) can be cloudy yet perfectly fine to drink.

• While looking at your wine, consider the colour. White wines develop a stronger colour as they age and turn from a pale yellow to a darker, warmer hue. Red wines, conversely, lose their colour. Younger reds are a deep purple or red and on ageing can become a tawny brown.

• Swirl the wine and watch the trails of wine, known as "legs", move down the inside of the glass. The more viscous the wine, the higher its alcohol content.

Aroma

• Swirling your glass aerates the wine. The oxidation that occurs frees the wine's "bouquet", revealing its complexity.

• Place your nose into the top of glass so you can fully capture the aromas in the bouquet.

• Wine aromas can broadly be grouped into fruit, spice, floral, vegetal, woody, animal, earthy, sweet, nutty and chemical.

• Once you know which aromas are commonly found in each type of wine, it becomes easier to identify the distinctive aromas in a particular wine. The wine aroma chart at page 147 will help you become familiar with the aromas of different grape varieties.

• If the wine smells of a damp, musty cellar or of wet cardboard then it is probably corked.

Taste

• At this stage you should take a sip of your wine.

• Whilst your nose can identify thousands of aromas, the tongue only detects five flavours: sweet, salt, acidity, bitterness and savoury (also known as "umami").

• As such, in order to fully appreciate a wine's complexity, you need to engage your sense of smell while you drink.

• Tilt your head down and take a sip of wine. While you still have the wine in your mouth, draw in air as if you are sipping through a straw. This makes a satisfying, albeit slightly inelegant, slurping noise.

• As well as identifying flavour, notice how long the taste of wine lingers. The quality of a wine is indicated by the longevity of its taste.

• Can you detect tannins? Tannins derive from grape skins, seeds and stalks and are found in red wine. They give structure to a wine but are also bitter and may cause your mouth to feel dry. Tannins mellow as wine ages so the most tannic wines are often young and full-bodied reds like those made from Tempranillo, Shiraz and Cabernet Sauvignon. Examples include Rioja and young reds from Piedmont, the Rhône and Bordeaux.

• A wine's "body" is described according to how it feels in the mouth. Light bodied wines, for example Pinot Noir and Beaujolais, feel fresh and delicate and do not have much tannin. Full-bodied wines are heavier, richer and have a higher alcohol content. Examples include an oaked Chardonnay and aged red Bordeaux.

• If your mouth waters then your tongue has identified a wine's acidity. If a wine does not have sufficient acidity to balance its other elements then it is described as "flabby".

WHITE GRAPE FLAVOURS

RIESLING	VIOGNIER	CHENIN BLANC
Passion fruit	Guava	Melon
Pineapple	Kiwi	Pineapple
Grapefruit	Tangerine	Lime
Lime	Apricot	Green apple
Apricot	Peach	Quince
Peach	Fig	Elderflower
Orange peel	Orange blossom	Grass
Rose petal	Violet	
Steel	Honeysuckle	
	Mint	

MATURING FLAVOURS

RIESLING	VIOGNIER	CHENIN BLANC
Honey	Honey	Honey
Toast	Butter	Almond
Clove	Hazelnut	Oak
Petrol	Oak	
	Toast	
	Smoke	

RED GRAPE FLAVOURS

PINOT NOIR	GRENACHE	MERLOT
Blackberry	Blackberry	Blackberry
Strawberry	Raspberry	Blackcurrant
Cherry	Cherry	Redcurrant
Plum	Plum	Plum
Beetroot	Undergrowth	Leaf
Black pepper	Black pepper	
Cinnamon	Liquorice	
Hay		

MATURING FLAVOURS

PINOT NOIR	GRENACHE	MERLOT
Vanilla	Prune	Nut
Farmyard	Chocolate	Sawdust
Clove	Smoke	Leather
Hay	Mineral	Clove
		Tobacco

GRAPE FLAVOURS

	CHAMPAGNE & SPARKLING WINE	SWEET WINE	PORT
W	Grapefruit	Mango	Blackberry (R)
	Lemon	Apricot	Blackcurrant
	Pear	Lychee	Black cherry
	Apple	Fig	Plum
	Quince	Floral	Truffle
	Floral	Honey	Pepper
	Patisserie	Butter	
Rs	Strawberry		
	Raspberry		
	Cherry		
	Floral		

MATURING FLAVOURS

	CHAMPAGNE & SPARKLING WINE	SWEET WINE	PORT
W	Yeast	Mandarin	Chocolate (R)
	Honey	Wax	Caramel
	Almond	Almond	Walnut
	Toast	Vanilla	Almond
Rs	Yeast	Lanolin	Coffee
	Hay		Smoke
			Vanilla

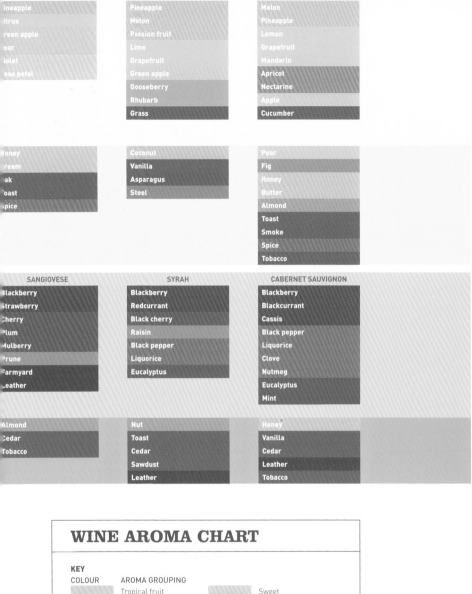

PINOT GRIS	SAUVIGNON BLANC	CHARDONNAY
Pineapple	Pineapple	Melon
Citrus	Melon	Pineapple
Green apple	Passion fruit	Lemon
Pear	Lime	Grapefruit
Violet	Grapefruit	Mandarin
Rose petal	Green apple	Apricot
	Gooseberry	Nectarine
	Rhubarb	Apple
	Grass	Cucumber

Honey	Coconut	Pear
Cream	Vanilla	Fig
Oak	Asparagus	Honey
Toast	Steel	Butter
Spice		Almond
		Toast
		Smoke
		Spice
		Tobacco

SANGIOVESE	SYRAH	CABERNET SAUVIGNON
Blackberry	Blackberry	Blackberry
Strawberry	Redcurrant	Blackcurrant
Cherry	Black cherry	Cassis
Plum	Raisin	Black pepper
Mulberry	Black pepper	Liquorice
Prune	Liquorice	Clove
Farmyard	Eucalyptus	Nutmeg
Leather		Eucalyptus
		Mint

Almond	Nut	Honey
Cedar	Toast	Vanilla
Tobacco	Cedar	Cedar
	Sawdust	Leather
	Leather	Tobacco

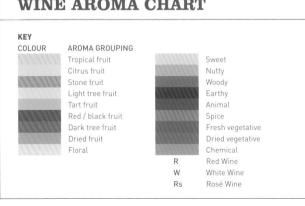

WINE AROMA CHART

KEY

COLOUR   AROMA GROUPING

Tropical fruit

Citrus fruit

Stone fruit

Light tree fruit

Tart fruit

Red / black fruit

Dark tree fruit

Dried fruit

Floral

Sweet

Nutty

Woody

Earthy

Animal

Spice

Fresh vegetative

Dried vegetative

Chemical

R   Red Wine

W   White Wine

Rs   Rosé Wine

Cheese & Wine Matching

The aim of cheese and wine matching is to find a combination that is better than the sum of its parts. Luckily, there are so many different cheeses and wines available that, with enough experimentation, you are bound to find a few stellar pairings.

All tasting is subjective so there are no right or wrong matches. Some combinations, however, are considered to work better than others. It is a common misconception that cheese should be paired with red wine. There are some wonderful red wine and cheese pairings but more often than not the tannins found in red wine overpower the softer, creamy elements of a cheese. Perhaps surprisingly, white wine is more versatile and a safer bet. Another general rule of thumb is that cheese and wine from the same region work well together.

If you are serving a few different types of cheese, you will be unlikely to find one wine which matches brilliantly with all of them. The most sensible approach is to choose a wine which creates a winning combination with one or two of the cheeses but does not clash with the others. Similarly, if your focus is one particular wine then choose a couple of cheeses that complement that wine.

Here are some brief guidance notes, which show how varied cheese and wine pairings can be. Try our suggestions or go off piste to create your own favourite combinations.

Fresh Cheese

Most fresh cheese has a delicate flavour so a light, white wine would match well. If you are serving a slightly acidic goat's milk cheese, such as Childwickbury or Perroche, try a New World Sauvignon Blanc - the tropical fruit and gooseberry notes of the wine, along with its acidity, balance the citrus flavour of the cheese.

Soft Cheese

The classic accompaniment to a mature goat's milk cheese is a French Sauvignon Blanc. The wine's dryness and subtle green fruit flavours complement a fresh and tangy cheese with goaty aroma. A dry, light rosé should also work well. Rich cheeses, such as Brillat-Savarin and La Tur, are fantastic with Champagne and Chardonnay. Try matching Saint-Marcellin with a fruity Côtes du Rhône.

Semi-Soft Cheese

In some ways, semi-soft cheeses are the easiest to pair because they can make a delicious match with white and red wines as well as sparkling wine. But in choosing a suitable wine it is important to consider the flavour and creaminess of the cheese. If you are looking to drink white wine then Chardonnay (including the sparkling Blanc de Blancs) is a good bet since its crispness can match well with a buttery cheese, whether it is mild or stronger flavoured. Chardonnay is not always a winner and other possible wines include New World Pinot Gris, white Burgundy, Viognier, Sancerre or dry Côtes de Provence rosé. If you fancy a red wine, a young Bordeaux or Burgundy can pair well with semi-soft cheeses, as can a Beaujolais and Pinot Noir. Robust reds, such as a New World Shiraz or Cabernet Sauvignon, will overpower these cheeses and should be avoided.

Hard Cheese

The cheeses in this category have diverse flavours, making them tough to match with wine in general terms. The key is to make sure that neither the cheese nor wine overpowers the other. For milder hard cheeses, like Morbier and Cornish Yarg, try an Alsace Riesling, a Chablis or a white Burgundy to enhance their flavour. A softer red,

such as a Valpolicella or Pinot Noir, could also work providing it does not overwhelm the subtle flavours of the cheese. A salty cheese will taste saltier with a high alcohol content wine but it will also bring out a wine's fruitiness and neutralise its acidity. For these cheeses, perhaps head for a mature and fruity Old World red with moderate tannins like a Chianti, Côtes du Rhône or Beaujolais. Alternatively, sweeter wines will balance the salt of the cheese and usually will work here. If the cheese is strong but less salty then it will stand up well to a Barolo, New World Shiraz, Merlot or mature Bordeaux. Champagne and softer Tempranillo make very different but interesting pairings with hard, ewe's milk cheese.

Blue Cheese

Sweet and fortified wines are the classic partners for blue cheese. Port is the traditional pairing for Stilton and Sauternes for Roquefort. Milder blue cheeses such as Gorgonzola Dolce, Fourme d'Ambert and Tomme Bluette Chèvre go well with aromatic white wines such as Riesling, Gewurztraminer, Zinfandel and Torrontés. Spicier blues like Picos de Europa and Gorgonzola Piccante could handle a robust regional red though you may prefer to go for something sweeter like Sherry or Muscat.

Washed Rind Cheese

Washed rind cheeses, such as Epoisses and Stinking Bishop, are notoriously difficult to match, particularly with red wine. If the rind has been washed in a wine, spirit or beer then that beverage should make a good pairing with the cheese. If you have a less pungent washed rind cheese like Chaumes then a fruity Bordeaux, Merlot or Beaujolais could pair well. Stronger cheeses like Reblochon, Ardrahan and Taleggio should work with a white Burgundy, German Riesling, Pinot Gris or unoaked Chardonnay. The meaty Menorcan cheese, Mahón, works famously well with Sherry.

CHEESE & WINE MATCHING TABLE

		CHEESE			
		SOFT			SEMI-SOFT
		Brillat-Savarin	Golden Cross	Valençay	Brie / Camembert	Serra da Estrela
WINE	Champagne	✓		✓	✓	
	Chardonnay	✓		✓	✓	✓
	Sweet Riesling		✓			
	Sauvignon Blanc	✓	✓	✓	✓	
	Beaujolais		✓	✓	✓	
	Bordeaux				✓	✓
	Merlot					✓
	Pinot Noir	✓			✓	
	Rioja					
	Muscadet			✓		
	Sauternes					
	Port					✓
	Ale / Porter / Stout					
	Cider					

Favourite combinations

Some of our favourite cheese and wine pairings include:

Beenleigh Blue and Cider

Carboncino and dry, Loire Valley rosé

Aged Gruyère and London Porter Ale

Munster and Gewürztraminer

Olde Remeker and California Cabernet Sauvignon

Payoyo and Torrontés

Stichelton and Monbazillac

Tomme Fleurette and dry, Alsace Riesling

Vacherin Mont d'Or and Prosecco

CHEESE							
HARD					WASHED RIND	BLUE	
Mature Cheddar	Comté	Manchego Curado	Parmigiano-Reggiano	Pecorino Sardo	Taleggio	Gorgonzola Dolce	Roquefort / Stilton
	✓				✓		
	✓			✓	✓	✓	
		✓				✓	
✓	✓					✓	✓
✓							
✓	✓			✓	✓		✓
✓		✓	✓				
	✓		✓	✓	✓		
	✓					✓	✓
✓		✓	✓	✓		✓	✓
✓		✓					✓
✓		✓					

Recipes

Baronet and Cauliflower Bavarois

by The Square

....

INGREDIENTS

150g Cauliflower

150ml Whipping cream

100ml Milk

Pinch of salt

2 Gelatine leaves

300g Baronet cheese (without the rind)

150ml Double cream

10 Seedless grapes, quartered

1 ½ Granny Smith apples, finely diced

1 ½ Sticks of celery, finely diced

10 Walnuts finely chopped

80ml Apple juice

50ml Walnut oil

½ tsp Sherry

Sourdough bread (as a serving accompaniment)

(Serves 5 as a starter)

....

METHOD

1. Finely shred the cauliflower and place into a pan. Cover with the whipping cream and milk and bring to the boil over a medium heat

2. Add a pinch of salt and cook at a bare simmer for 5 minutes

3. Soften the gelatine leaves in cold water

4. Remove the cauliflower from the heat, add the Baronet and gelatine

5. Set aside for 5 minutes to allow the cheese to soften and then blitz to a smooth purée in a blender

6. Pass through a fine sieve and set aside to cool slightly

7. Whisk the double cream to soft peaks and fold into the Baronet mix

8. Divide the mix between 5 small bowls. Place in the fridge to set

9. Combine all the remaining ingredients and spoon the resulting dressing over the top of the mousses

10. Serve with sourdough bread

Cheddar and Bacon Bread and Butter Pudding

by The Cheese and Wine Company

·····································

INGREDIENTS

60g Finely chopped smoked bacon or lardons

1 ½ Slices of traditionally made white bread

Butter, enough to spread thickly on the bread

50g Grated mature Cheddar cheese

1 Spring onion, chopped

1 Egg

50ml Double cream

Cracked black pepper

(Serves 2 as a small dish)

···

METHOD

1. Pre-heat oven to 180°C fan assisted oven or 200°C conventional oven
2. Dry fry the bacon or lardons until lightly crisp
3. Butter the bread thickly and place in a small ovenproof dish. Sprinkle the bacon over the bread
4. Add the grated mature Cheddar and a small handful of chopped spring onions
5. Whisk the egg with the double cream and pour over the filled dish
6. Bake for around ten minutes until it has risen and is golden on top

Chez Bruce's Parmesan Biscuits

by Chez Bruce

···

INGREDIENTS

Small pinch of baking powder

Small pinch of smoked paprika

Small pinch of cayenne pepper

Large pinch of salt

85g Unsalted butter, softened

90g Grated Parmesan cheese

Black pepper to season

105g Plain flour

Black onion seeds, sesame seeds, caraway seeds and Maldon sea salt to roll

(Makes around 20 biscuits)

···

METHOD

1. Pre-heat oven to 140°C fan assisted oven or 160°C conventional oven

2. Beat together all the ingredients except the flour and seed mix. This is easiest and most effective if the butter is very soft

3. Mix in the flour. Do not work the mixture too much at this point

4. Roll the biscuit dough into a log. The diameter of the log will be the width of the finished biscuits

5. Roll the log in the seed mix. Chill in the fridge until firm

6. Slice biscuits off the log about 4mm thick with a serrated knife

7. Bake for about 10 minutes or until golden

8. Serve with Champagne!

Griddled Nectarine with Monte Enebro and English Speck

by Hamish Johnston

....

INGREDIENTS

3 Nectarines

150g Monte Enebro cheese

6 Slices of English speck

75g Rocket

3 tbsp Olive oil

1 tbsp Runny honey

Salt and pepper to season

Extra olive oil for griddle

(Serves 4 as a small dish or side salad)

....

METHOD

1. Remove the nectarine stones and cut each nectarine into quarters. Brush with olive oil and griddle over a low-medium heat until slightly softened and char lines appear

2. Whilst the nectarines are cooking, prepare the rest of the ingredients. Wash the rocket, tear the speck into pieces and crumble the cheese

3. Make the simple dressing by whisking the olive oil and honey together and seasoning with salt and pepper

4. When the nectarines are ready, toss the salad lightly together and drizzle with the dressing

Old Winchester Soufflé

by The Cheeseboard

....

INGREDIENTS

40g Unsalted butter

30g Plain flour

Pinch of English mustard powder

290ml Whole milk

70g - 100g Old Winchester cheese, coarsely grated (modify to taste)

4 eggs, separated

Salt and pepper to season

Knob of extra butter for greasing the ramekins

Breadcrumbs to line the ramekins

(Serves 6)

....

METHOD

1. Pre-heat oven to 180°C fan assisted oven or 200°C conventional oven

2. Place a baking tray on a shelf in the top third of the oven

3. Grease each ramekin with butter and sprinkle liberally with breadcrumbs to cover the whole dish, tap out any excess

4. Melt the butter, then stir in the flour and mustard powder. Cook for 45 seconds

5. Add the milk gradually whilst continuously stirring until the smooth mixture reaches boiling point

6. Boil for 2 minutes, whilst stirring. The mixture will get quite thick.

7. Remove from the heat and spoon the mixture into a large bowl. Then stir in the cheese

8. Once the mixture has cooled slightly, add the egg yolks and season well with salt and pepper

9. Whisk the egg whites to a medium peak in a clean bowl. Add one tablespoon of this to your cheese mix and beat well to loosen the mix

10. Fold in the rest of the egg whites quickly and efficiently, knocking out as little air as possible

11. Spoon the mixture into each ramekin, until filled two-thirds of the way up

12. Place the ramekins on the pre-heated baking tray in the oven and cook for 7 - 9 minutes. They will be ready when only a slight wobble is left

13. Serve immediately

Pork, Thyme and Taleggio Pizza

by The Deli Downstairs

....

INGREDIENTS

1/2 Sachet of dried yeast

1/2 tsp Sugar

150ml Luke warm water

200g '00' Flour or strong white bread flour

50g Semolina flour

1/2 tsp Salt

1/4 tbsp Olive oil

1/4 tbsp Milk

100g Left over roast pork

100g Taleggio cheese

1 Sprig of thyme, leaves only

4 - 5 tbsp Tomato sauce

35g Rocket

Juice of half a lemon

(Makes 1 pizza, 12 inch diameter)

....

METHOD

1. Mix together the yeast, sugar and water
2. In a separate large bowl, mix together both flours and the salt
3. Create a well in the centre of the flour mix. Once the yeast mix begins to bubble, pour this into the well with the olive oil and milk
4. When the mixture holds together, tip it onto a floured work surface
5. Knead the dough for 10 minutes until smooth, soft and springy
6. Place the dough in a lightly oiled bowl and cover with a damp tea towel. Leave in a warm place until double in size. This takes between 30 minutes and an hour
7. Pre-heat oven to 200°C fan assisted oven or 220°C conventional oven
8. Roll out the dough then cover with the tomato sauce topped with the pork, Taleggio, thyme and rocket. Squeeze over the lemon juice
9. Cook for 15 - 25 minutes, until the dough is crisp and golden brown and the cheese has melted

The Ledbury Cheese on Toast

by The Ledbury

· ·

INGREDIENTS

Croque Mix

300g Béchamel mix

40g Egg yolk

35g Parmesan cheese

50g Saint-Nectaire cheese

Salt and pepper to season

4 Slices of good bread

Butter for frying

Béchamel Mix

800ml Milk

1 Sprig of thyme

125g Butter

125g Plain flour

Pinch of Maldon sea salt

(Makes 4 slices)

· ·

METHOD

1. Place milk and thyme in a pan and bring to the simmer, remove from the heat and leave to infuse for 10 minutes

2. Melt the butter in a separate pan, stir in the flour and cook for 1 minute stirring continuously. Do not let the mixture brown

3. Remove from the heat and stir in the infused milk, a little at a time until the mixture is smooth (remove thyme sprig beforehand)

4. Return to the heat and stir continuously until the mixture reaches boiling point

5. Continue cooking and stirring for 2 minutes

6. Season with Maldon sea salt

7. Allow the béchamel to cool slightly then add the egg yolk, Parmesan and Saint-Nectaire. Mix until smooth and season to taste with salt and pepper

8. Melt the rest of the butter in a pan and fry the bread until golden and crisp

9. Add the Croque mix on top of the toast and grill for 1 minute until warm through and golden

Traditional Welsh Rarebit

by Daylesford Organic Farmshop & Café

....

INGREDIENTS

6 Slices of sourdough bread

450g Welsh Rarebit mix

Handful of mixed salad leaves

Salad dressing to taste

Daylesford chutney

Welsh Rarebit Mix

350g Cheddar cheese, coarsely grated

80ml Milk

20g English mustard

25g Plain four

10ml Worcestershire sauce

1 Egg

1 Egg yolk

Salt and pepper

(Makes 6 Welsh Rarebits)

....

METHOD

Rarebit Mix

1. Place the cheese in a pan with the milk and melt
2. Add the mustard, flour and Worcestershire sauce. Stir until incorporated, then take off the heat and allow to cool slightly
3. Beat the whole egg and egg yolk together, then add to the rest of the mix and beat in vigorously. Season with the salt and pepper
4. Leave to cool. This mix can be made well in advance
5. Pre-heat oven to 180°C fan assisted oven or 200°C conventional oven
6. Slice the sourdough and spread with the Rarebit mixture. Place on a tray and cook for 8 minutes until golden brown and slightly crispy underneath
7. Place on a small plate and garnish with a pile of dressed salad leaves and a spoon of chutney

Cheese Glossary

Affinage (Fr.): The process of maturing cheese

Affineur (Fr.): A person who matures cheese

Artisan cheese: Small-scale, locally produced cheese of high quality, often made using traditional methods with minimal mechanisation

Bloomy rind: The velvety rind found on many semi-soft cheeses, such as Brie de Meaux and Camembert

Cheesemonger: A person who sells cheese

Cloth binding: A traditional English method of making cheese, for example Cheddar, Cheshire and Wensleydale

Cooked cheese:
1. Cheese which has been made by heating the milk before the curds are put into moulds, to encourage the draining of whey

2. Melted cheese

Creamery: An establishment where milk is pasteurised and/or cheese is made

Curd: The solids that form when milk curdles

Curdling: The process by which curd separates from whey, triggered by the introduction of rennet

Farmhouse cheese: Cheese which is made on the cheesemaker's farm using milk exclusively from his or her own animals

Fromage (Fr.): Cheese

Fromager (Fr.): A cheesemonger or cheesemaker

Maturing: The process of ageing cheese in temperature and humidity controlled conditions until it reaches its optimum texture and flavour. Also known as ripening

Mould:
1. Microscopic fungi found on the outside or inside of cheese

2. A container into which curd is scooped or layered to encourage whey to drain. The finished cheese will be the same shape and size of the mould

Paste or pate: The interior part of the cheese, from underneath the rind to the centre of the cheese

Pasteurisation: The process by which milk is heated to destroy harmful micro-organisms

PDO: Stands for Protected Designation of Origin and is the European Union mark of origin

Pressing: A process during cheesemaking where a weight is pressed down on the curd to extract excess whey

Raw milk: Milk which has not been pasteurised

Rennet: A substance added to milk to initiate curdling. Rennet derives from the fourth stomach lining of young ruminants (traditionally, calves) or is made from a vegetable product such as thistles, nettles or fig leaves

Rind: The outside layer of a cheese

Ripening: See "Maturing"

Triple-cream cheese: Cheese which has a high butterfat content, giving it an intensely rich and creamy taste

Triple milk cheese: Cheese made with milk from goats, ewes and cows. These cheeses are typical of the Piedmont region in Italy but are made throughout Europe

Truckle: A tall cylinder of cheese, usually English, for example Cheddar or Stilton

Territorial cheese: British cheese that takes its name from the region in which it has been made. Examples include Cheshire, Lancashire, Red Leicester and Wensleydale cheeses

Turophile: A connoisseur or lover of cheese

Unpasteurised cheese: Cheese made from raw milk

Vegetarian cheese: Cheese made with a non-animal rennet

Washed rind cheese: Cheese that is regularly washed in brine, often mixed with wine or spirits, during the maturing process. The rind develops a pinkish-orangey-brown colour and becomes sticky. Washed rind cheeses tend to have a pungent aroma

Waxed paper: Speciality paper for wrapping cut cheese which stops the cheese from drying out quickly whilst allowing it to breathe, thereby minimising the build up of moisture

Wheel: A relatively flat disc of whole cheese, for example Gouda or Gruyère

Whey: The liquid that forms when milk curdles

Wine Glossary

....

Ageing: Storing young wine for a period of time until it reaches its optimum drinking condition. Also known as cellaring, laying down or maturing

Aroma: The smell of a wine. Also known as the wine's bouquet or nose

Bin: A wine storage area

Bin End: The last of a merchant's stock of a particular wine

Biodynamic Wine: Wine which is made following the principles of "biodynamism", founded by the Austrian philosopher Rudolf Steiner in the 1920s. This is the belief that lunar movements and constellations affect the quality of agricultural produce. Biodynamic winemakers choose the best days to sow, plant, harvest and bottle based on an astrological calendar. The calendar also indicates good and bad days for drinking wine

Blend: Wine made from a combination of grape varieties

Blind Tasting: Tasting a wine without knowing in advance what it is. Professionals conduct blind tastings so they can judge a wine on its merits, without being prejudiced by the wine's label

Bouquet: The complex aroma of a wine

Brut (Fr.): "Dry" in a sparkling wine. Used in Champagne and other styles

Case: Either six or 12 bottles, usually of the same wine, bought together

Cellaring: See "Ageing"

Cork: Natural cork is made from tree bark and is the traditional material used to seal a bottle. The most well-known problem with natural cork is called "cork taint", which adversely affects the flavour of the wine

Corked: Wine which is tainted by the chemical trichloranisole (TCA), found in the cork. The chemical is harmless but corked wine has the unpleasant odour of a damp or mouldy cellar

Cork Taint: See "Corked"

Cru (Fr.): A particularly high quality wine, for example "grand cru" or "premier cru"

Cuvée (Fr.): An individual barrel, blend or style of wine within an estate's portfolio

Decanting: Pouring wine from the bottle into a secondary container, known as a decanter. This aerates the wine, allowing its full aroma and flavour to develop, and it also separates the wine from any sediment at the bottom of the bottle. Wine is then poured from the decanter into a wine glass

Demi-Sec (Fr.): Medium dry wine

Double decanting: Pouring a decanted wine back into its original wine bottle so the bottle's label is visible when the wine is served

En Primeur (Fr.): The sale of wine before it is bottled, often for investment purposes

Enomatic Wine Sampling Machine:
A unit which preserves an open
bottle of wine for around two to three
weeks and dispenses different sized
measures of wine to facilitate
wine tasting

Enoteca (It.): An Italian wine shop
or bar. The literal translation is
"wine repository"

Estate Bottled Champagne: See
"Grower Champagne"

Estate Wine: Wine made from
grapes grown only on the
winemaker's property

Flabby: A wine which has insufficient
acidity to balance its other elements

Flight: Several different wines,
presented together, to create a wine
tasting experience

Fortified Wine: Wine to which
brandy has been added during the
winemaking process. Fortified wines
have an alcohol content of around
17% - 21%. If brandy is added before
the fermentation process then the
fortified wine is sweet. If brandy is
added afterwards then the wine is
dry. Examples include Port, Sherry,
Madeira and Marsala

Full Bodied: Wines which are heavy or
rich on the palate and have a relatively
high alcohol content

Grape Variety: A type of grape such as
Sauvignon Blanc, Merlot, Pinot Gris,
Zinfandel, Chardonnay, Syrah etc.

Grower Champagne: Champagne
made by the same estate that has
grown the grapes. Also known as
estate bottled Champagne

Laying Down: Storing young wine for
a period of time until it reaches its
optimum drinking condition. The term
derives from the horizontal position
in which the wine is kept during the
ageing process. This prevents the cork
from drying out and shrinking, which
could spoil the wine

Legs: The trails of wine which run
down the inside of a glass after
swirling. The slower the wine runs
downs the inside of the glass, the
higher the alcohol content of the wine

Master of Wine: A person who has
been awarded a qualification by the
Institute of Masters of Wine. The title
demonstrates the highest level of
expertise in the industry. There are
only around 300 Masters of Wine in
the world

Maturing: See "Ageing"

Merchant: Someone who sells wine.
Also known as a vintner

Mixed Case: Six or 12 bottles of
different wines bought together

Must: Grape juice before or during the
fermentation process

Natural Wine: Wine made with
minimal technological intervention
and chemicals. Natural wine is often

Wine Glossary contd.

made without the addition of sulphites or by adding only a small amount of sulphites. The wine can be cloudy, slightly fizzy and/or an unusual colour, for example white natural wines can be a dark orange colour. The quality of natural wine can be variable

New World Wine: Wine made outside the traditional European winemaking regions. New World winemaking regions include South Africa, Chile, Argentina, California, Australia and New Zealand etc.

Nose: See "Aroma"

Oak-aged: Wine that has been aged in oak barrels. The oak softens the wine's tannins and imparts certain flavours, particularly vanilla and toasted notes. The origin of the oak, whether French, American or Eastern European, will affect the flavour of the wine

Oenophile: A wine lover or connoisseur

Old World Wine: Wine grown and made in the traditional European winemaking regions: France, Germany, Italy, Spain, Portugal and Central/Eastern Europe

Organic Wine: Wines made from grapes grown without artificial additives or enhancers and in accordance with organic farming rules

Oxidation: This occurs when the wine is exposed to air, most frequently when a bottle has been left open or aged for too long. The wine develops a brown or yellow tinge and smells of vinegar

Punt: The indentation at the base of a wine bottle

Reserve: This may indicate a superior or aged wine but there are no legal requirements for labelling a wine as Reserve and the description is no guarantee of quality

Sommelier (Fr.): A specialist wine waiter or steward

Sulphite: Sulphur Dioxide found in wine. Sulphites are added during the winemaking process to destroy yeast and bacteria and to protect the wine from oxidation

Tannin: A chemical compound released from grape skins, seeds and stems during pressing and found in red wine. Tannins add structure and body to wine but have an astringent flavour and often cause the mouth to feel dry

Terroir: The essence of a region. Certain characteristics of a region's soil and climate impart distinctive flavour and aroma to produce from that region

Vinification: The process of winemaking, starting with the selection of grapes

Vintage: The year in which grapes are grown and harvested

Vintage Wine: Wine made from grapes that were all or primarily grown and harvested in a single year

Vintner: A winemaker or merchant

Viticulture: Grape-growing and farming

A-Z List of Venues

A-Z List of Venues contd.